ANNUAL UPDATE 20

UK GOVERNMENT & POLITICS

Neil McNaughton

Eric Magee

PHILIP ALLAN FOR

HODDER
EDUCATION

AN HACHETTE UK COMPANY

Philip Allan, an imprint of Hodder Education, an Hachette UK company,
Blenheim Court, George Street, Banbury, Oxfordshire OX16 5BH

Orders

Bookpoint Ltd, 130 Park Drive, Milton Park, Abingdon, Oxfordshire OX14 4SE
tel: 01235 827827
fax: 01235 400401
e-mail: education@bookpoint.co.uk

Lines are open 9.00 a.m.–5.00 p.m., Monday to Saturday, with a 24-hour
message answering service. You can also order through the Hodder Education
website: www.hoddereducation.co.uk

© Neil McNaughton and Eric Magee 2016

ISBN 978-1-4718-6795-8

First printed 2016

Impression number 5 4 3 2 1

Year 2020 2019 2018 2017 2016

436913
320.941 (McN)

Typeset by Integra Software Services Pvt. Ltd., Pondicherry, India

Cover photo: Kevin Smart/iStock

Printed by CPI Group (UK) Ltd, Croydon CR0 4YY

Hachette UK's policy is to use papers that are natural, renewable and recyclable
products and made from wood grown in sustainable forests. The logging
and manufacturing processes are expected to conform to the environmental
regulations of the country of origin.

Contents

Chapter 1

Jeremy Corbyn: a new kind of politics?

Context

Ed Miliband resigned as party leader shortly after Labour's election defeat in May 2015. While he was Labour Party leader he changed the procedures for electing the party leader. There had been widespread criticism of the old system on the grounds that it put too much power into the hands of trade unions and MPs (Ed Miliband beat his brother David in 2010 largely because of union support).

The very start of the process began in a strange way. Under the rules a candidate must receive at least 35 nominations from Labour MPs. This is to prevent frivolous candidacies from people with no chance of victory. It was therefore a deep irony that Jeremy Corbyn, the ultimate winner, appeared unlikely at first to receive 35 nominations. However, some members of the party believed that his very left-wing views ought to be heard during the leadership contest. He therefore received nominations from MPs who were *not* his supporters, merely to ensure that his voice was heard and that internal democracy would be better served. One of these was Margaret Beckett, a former deputy leader of the party and very much a 'Blairite' moderate. Once it became clear that Corbyn might actually win, she said she regretted nominating him.

The election system

The following are eligible to vote:

- full members of the Labour Party
- members of trade unions who have dual membership with the party and members of affiliated organisations such as the Fabian Society and the Co-operative movement

- a new group of people who can pay £3 and register as 'Labour Party supporters', but not members. This proved to be controversial as it might open the door to people whose views were not compatible with existing Labour policies or even political opponents intent on making mischief by voting for potentially unpopular candidates

All votes are of equal weight, i.e. one person, one vote. The electoral system used is known as **alternative vote** (the system rejected in a 2011 referendum after it was proposed as the new system to elect Westminster MPs). It can be described as a **preferential** and also as a **majority** system in that voters can show more than one preference and the final winner will have over 50% of the votes. This system works as follows:

- Voters place the candidates in order of preference.
- The first preference votes are counted. Any candidate who receives over 50% of these votes is automatically elected. (This is what actually happened in this case with Corbyn winning almost 60% of first preferences.)
- If no candidate achieves over 50% of first preferences, the bottom candidate drops out (in this election that *would have been* Liz Kendall, but it did not come to that). This losing candidate's second preferences are added to the other candidates. Again if any candidate now has over 50% of the votes, he or she is elected.
- If no candidate still has an absolute majority, the new bottom candidate drops out (this would have been Yvette Cooper) and their second preferences are added to each candidate. Again anyone with a 50% + 1 majority is elected.
- This continues until there are only two candidates, so one of them must, by definition, achieve an absolute majority.

The significance of this system is that, had Corbyn not achieved an overall majority, or very close to it, on first preferences, he might have struggled to win as he might have won very few second preference votes. But, as we know, this was not the case, such was the scale of his victory.

The result and its significance

There is no point here in detailing the full result as the election did not go beyond first preferences. Table 1.1 therefore only shows first preference votes.

Table 1.1 The total first preference votes for Labour leadership candidates, September 2015

Candidate	Total votes	% of first preferences *
Jeremy Corbyn	251,417	59.5
Andy Burnham	80,462	19.0
Yvette Cooper	71,928	17.0
Liz Kendall	18,857	4.5

*Rounded up or down

Equally interesting is the result broken down according to types of voter. This is shown in Table 1.2.

Table 1.2 Labour leadership result by types of voter

Candidate	% full members	% associated members	% registered supporters
Jeremy Corbyn	49.6	57.6	83.8
Andy Burnham	22.7	26.0	5.8
Yvette Cooper	22.2	12.6	8.0
Liz Kendall	5.5	3.7	2.4

In all, 422,871 people voted — a turnout of 76.3%.

- This was a very large electorate with over 400,000 people voting. No other internal party elections approach anywhere near this figure.
- Obviously it was a strikingly big win for Corbyn, leaving no room for doubt about his election.
- A key statistic shows that he won virtually 50% of the votes of full party members (i.e. not including people who simply paid £3 for the right to vote). This means he would have won in a conventional election.
- Corbyn won the vast majority of the votes of the registered supporters. This suggests that a large number of people who might not normally participate in politics were inspired sufficiently to take part. Some of these may well now become full party members and so arrest the long-term decline in party membership.
- Liz Kendall, a self-confessed 'Blairite', was soundly beaten, demonstrating the degree to which the ideas of Tony Blair are now discredited.

Nevertheless, a major problem is now faced by the Labour Party. As this was a 'one person, one vote' election, the MPs had no special status. Their votes were of equal value to ordinary members. The fact that Corbyn could not originally secure 35 nominations from MPs demonstrates the fact that he certainly does not enjoy the support of the vast majority of the parliamentary party. Thus, he may have great popularity in the country, but not in Parliament. Put another way, he has received a powerful **mandate** from the Labour electorate, but may have relatively little ability to carry it out.

Two other recent events are noteworthy and will affect the party's prospects. The first was the election of Sadiq Khan as the party's candidate in the elections for London mayor in May 2016. Khan is on the moderate left of the party and again demonstrates the change in the political sentiments of the membership who voted for him. The other was Tom Watson's election as deputy leader in the same election as that which elevated Corbyn to the leadership. Watson is radical on the issue of corporate tax avoidance, but is generally moderate.

Who is Jeremy Corbyn?

As a young man in the late 1970s and 1980s Corbyn was a left-wing activist who worked with trade unions and in local government in London. He was associated in his early political career with such well-known left wingers as Ken Livingstone and Tony Benn. He entered Parliament in 1983, the year of Labour's biggest election defeat in modern history, sitting for Islington North, a relatively deprived area in north London and a safe Labour seat. He has held the seat ever since.

Corbyn has supported many international movements dedicated to the overthrow of dictatorial regimes. He supported Irish republicanism in its struggle for a united Ireland. He also supports the Palestinian cause in the Middle East. Known as a Labour rebel, he is said to have defied his own party whip on hundreds of occasions, most notably voting against military intervention in Iraq in 2003. He is considered a conscientious constituency MP, a good, though unremarkable, speaker and, until 2015, appeared to have no special political ambitions.

As a now senior politician he is unusual in a number of ways:
- At 66 he is relatively old to be taking up such a senior position.
- He is modestly educated only to A-level standard and has no university degree (though John Major, prime minister from 1990 to 1997, also had little formal education).
- He lives a frugal life, makes virtually no expenses claims in Parliament, does not drive a car (he cycles), and is teetotal and a vegetarian.
- He is reputed to have split with his second wife over her decision to send one of their sons to a selective school, a system in which he does not believe. This indicates that he lives by his principles.
- He has never held any post of responsibility in the Labour Party.

Corbyn is unusual in a number of other ways too. He presents himself as a departure from the traditional image of a modern politician. He does not use spin doctors (though in his second week he did employ two advisers), he says what he believes rather than what he thinks other people or the media want him to say, he does not concern himself too much with his personal physical image and he has vowed to change the way he conducts politics. In his first appearance at Prime Minister's Question Time, he asked questions sent to him by ordinary citizens via e-mails and Twitter and he refused to engage in a shouting match, speaking quietly and firmly but never engaging in excessive argumentation.

This 'alternative' image may well turn out to be both an advantage and a disadvantage. It helps him in that he can appeal to the many people who are disillusioned with slick, stage-managed, metropolitan politics and politicians who speak in platitudes and sound bites. He looks authentic and stands up for what he believes. Even people who do not agree with many of his policies seem to respect him. This gives him a special appeal to the young, despite his age (Box 1.1). On the other hand, he is open to charges from the media that he cannot cope with modern politics, that he is naive and is out of touch with middle England.

Box 1.1 **Charlotte Church on Jeremy Corbyn**

The singer and political activist Charlotte Church said:

> There is something inherently virtuous about him, and that is a quality that can rally the support of a lot of people, and most importantly, a lot of young people.

What does Corbyn stand for?

In many ways Jeremy Corbyn is a classical **democratic socialist** and that is often how he describes himself and his close followers. This means he espouses policies that were popular in the Labour Party in the immediate period after the First World War and in the 1970s and 1980s. Such socialists believe in the power of the state to achieve social justice through welfare and the redistribution of income through taxation. They are also deeply suspicious of free market capitalism and believe that, while it can be tolerated, it must be strongly regulated. In that sense many see him as a throwback to a bygone age. Others argue more positively that his ideas are an appropriate response to the 'excesses' of modern capitalism and that he represents sections of society that have largely been ignored by parties and politicians in recent times.

Table 1.3 summarises Corbyn's main policies and shows how they differ from 'mainstream' Labour policies since the 1990s.

Table 1.3 Corbyn's policies compared to 'mainstream' Labour policies

Corbyn's main ideas	Mainstream Labour equivalent
The railways and energy companies should be nationalised and brought under state control	No new nationalisations. Instead industries should remain in the private sector but be regulated by the state to prevent exploitation of consumers
Taxes on the very wealthy should be increased. There will be draconian measures to eliminate tax evasion and avoidance particularly by large corporations	Modest increases in taxes on the wealthy should be considered
There should be more 'quantitative easing' (basically printing more money) to finance infrastructure projects such as railways, schools and hospitals. This will, he believes, stimulate growth and reduce the budget deficit without the need for cuts in government spending on benefits and services	Quantitative easing is inflationary and should be used with great caution if at all. The reduction of the deficit will have to mean cuts in public spending
There should be substantial increases in the level of the minimum (living) wage	Rises in the minimum wage should be in line with wage increases in general
The welfare cuts made under the coalition and proposed by the current government should be reversed	Labour supports the need for welfare benefit cuts but slightly less than Conservative proposals

Table 1.3 Corbyn's policies compared to 'mainstream' Labour policies (Continued)

Corbyn's main ideas	Mainstream Labour equivalent
There should be large increases in public spending on health and education. The state should build hundreds of thousands of new houses at accessible prices for both subsidised rent and purchase	Increased spending on health and education should be roughly in line with inflation. Modest proposals for house building, mostly for purchase
The renewal of the Trident nuclear weapon system should be cancelled and Britain should not have nuclear weapons at all	Britain should remain a nuclear power and renew Trident
Britain should consider withdrawing from NATO and should certainly have no involvement in Middle East affairs	Britain's place is firmly within NATO. A pragmatic approach to foreign military involvement
He has an ambivalent attitude to membership of the EU. If a better deal cannot be negotiated he would consider withdrawal	Labour is firmly pro EU
He wishes to see trade union rights, eroded since the 1980s, restored to their pre-1982 level	Labour does not support the restoration of union rights

The short-term aftermath of Corbyn's election

Not surprisingly, in the days and weeks following Corbyn's election there was considerable dismay among most senior Labour politicians. Their main emotion was that a party led by Corbyn which proposed his policies would be wiped out at the next general election (Box 1.2). As an indication of their discontent, a substantial group immediately indicated that they would not serve in a shadow cabinet. Among them were:

- **Tristram Hunt**, former shadow health secretary
- **Yvette Cooper**, defeated leadership candidate and former shadow home secretary
- **Mary Creagh**, former shadow secretary for international development
- **Chuka Umunna**, former shadow business secretary
- **Jamie Reed**, former shadow health minister
- **Rachel Reeves**, former shadow minister for work and pensions
- **Emma Reynolds**, former shadow minister for communities and local government
- **Liz Kendall**, defeated leadership candidate

Box 1.2 **Tony Blair on Jeremy Corbyn**

Tony Blair on the prospect of Jeremy Corbyn being elected Labour leader:

If Jeremy Corbyn becomes leader it won't be a defeat like 1983 or 2015 at the next election. It will mean rout, possibly annihilation.

Two groups opposed to Corbyn's leadership have already appeared in the Labour Party. Led by Umunna and Hunt, there is a group titling itself **Labour for the Common Good**, dedicated to promoting moderate policies along the lines of New Labour ideas. Among backbenchers there is a looser group called the **Resistance**, which has similar aims to Labour for the Common Good.

This suggests that the fault lines in Labour are already beginning to appear. Corbyn has attempted to unite the party with his shadow cabinet appointments, but he still faces an uphill struggle to keep the party behind him.

Notable shadow cabinet appointments were as follows:

- **John McDonnell, shadow chancellor of the exchequer.** This was the most dramatic and controversial appointment. McDonnell is even more left wing than Corbyn and has been equally rebellious in his parliamentary career. He supports the introduction of a 60% tax rate for people earning over £100,000 per annum and the nationalisation of the banks. He also does not accept any policies designed to reduce the public deficit that involve cuts in public expenditure. In the past he has declared himself as simply 'anti-capitalist'. Opponents say that McDonnell will convince the electorate that Labour will be economically irresponsible.
- **Diana Abbott, shadow international development secretary.** Abbott is another veteran left winger and a regular rebel against the party line. She is a natural Corbyn supporter.
- **Hilary Benn, shadow foreign secretary.** Benn is a surprise appointment as he stands in the centre of the party. He will help to bridge the gap with the centre of the party. This may be an appointment made out of personal loyalty as Corbyn used to be a political aide to his father, Tony Benn.
- **Andy Burnham, shadow home secretary.** Accepting Corbyn's olive branch, Burnham is slightly left of centre and so may be able to live with Corbyn's policies. Like Benn he is a key figure in the attempt to unite the party.
- **Chris Bryant, shadow leader of the House of Commons.** Bryant is another unifying appointment. However, Bryant has said he disagrees with Corbyn on many issues so it is difficult to see how he can stay in the shadow cabinet.
- **Rosie Winterton, chief whip.** She is already chief whip and will have the hardest job of all, trying to keep the party together on vital issues.
- **Angela Eagle, shadow business secretary.** One of two twins in the leadership group, she is left of centre and so a natural ally of Corbyn. She will stand in for Corbyn at Prime Minister's Question Time when he is absent. She will have a hard job persuading business leaders that the party has not become anti-business under Corbyn.

- **Maria Eagle, shadow defence secretary.** Maria is Angela's twin sister. A serious problem with her appointment will occur soon when Parliament has to vote on the renewal of the Trident nuclear system. Corbyn is opposed to renewal but Eagle has been in favour in the past. This will be a key test of her loyalty.
- **Michael Dugher, shadow culture secretary.** An Ed Miliband supporter, he will have difficulty supporting Corbyn's more radical policies.

Despite his attempts to unify the party, not least through his shadow cabinet appointments, Corbyn faces a number of immediate problems. Among them are these:

- His leadership team is inexperienced and many are almost totally unknown.
- If he tries to impose **collective responsibility** on his shadow cabinet, whereby all members will be required to support party policy, he will face real difficulties as so many of them do not agree with his fundamental ideas.
- He will have to decide which of his own beliefs he may be willing to sacrifice in the interests of party unity.
- He cannot count on the support of a large number of his own MPs.
- There are powerful individuals now on the backbenches who may well begin to plot his downfall.
- He may therefore face an early challenge to his leadership.
- The Labour Party faces two early tests for its new identity. These are the elections to the Scottish parliament and for the mayor of London, both in May 2016. If the party does badly in these elections, Corbyn will come under immediate pressure to stand down.

The potential long-term aftermath of Corbyn's election

The most dramatic scenario imaginable is a complete realignment of UK politics on the centre-left. This may involve the division of the Labour Party into two parts. One would be effectively a 'socialist' party, looking more like left-wing parties in other parts of Europe such as Greece and Spain, while the other would embrace the 'post Blairite' moderate elements that currently constitute the majority of the parliamentary party. There is a precedent for this kind of split. In the 1980s the Labour Party under Michael Foot's leadership adopted a series of left-wing policies not unlike those held currently by Corbyn (indeed this was the time when Corbyn entered Parliament in 1983). Many party members saw this as a serious error and broke away to form the Social Democratic Party (SDP). The SDP went on to amalgamate with the Liberals to form the current Liberal Democrat Party. It took Labour 15 years to recover from the trauma.

A second potential scenario is equally dramatic. This is that, in the long run, Corbyn will ignite a new political movement in the UK and that this movement will steadily grow into a major force. It might politicise many people who are currently disillusioned with traditional politics, particularly the young who are traditionally more radical in their views. Of course, to achieve electoral success this would have to be much larger than the quarter of a million people who voted for Corbyn in the leadership election. The first-past-the-post election system is a major barrier to the success of a new left-wing movement. This is because its support (rather like UKIP's) would be too dispersed to win many parliamentary seats. The victory of the radical SNP in Scotland in 2015 was the kind of phenomenon that could be replicated in parts of England.

At the time of the Labour Party annual conference at the end of September 2015, Corbyn argued that it was perfectly possible to debate policies and to come to decisions with which members of the shadow cabinet did not agree, for example over Trident renewal or whether to join the 'staying in' side in the EU referendum. This may certainly prove possible while Labour is in opposition and the next general election is distant. However, it is difficult to see how the party could fight an election in 5 years' time without a set of policies upon which *all* its potential ministers agree.

Many neutrals and Conservatives will take a simpler view of the long term. This is that the UK is destined to be dominated by conservatism for generations. The left, they argue, is too fragmented to recover and a new centre-right consensus will dominate for many years to come.

Summary

Some have argued that Labour had already lost its way before Corbyn was elected. This suggests that the party not only no longer appeals to 'middle England' but has also lost the support of the poorer and more deprived sections of society — its traditional supporters. Its defeat in most of the English constituencies and in Scotland in 2015 points to this conclusion. Those who support Corbyn and his policies subscribe to this view, suggesting that his election will actually *find* Labour's way again, that he appeals to Labour's core supporters such as young radicals, trade unionists, ethnic minorities and poorer communities. The problem is that this group of potential supporters is not numerous enough to be converted into a parliamentary majority at a general election.

Corbyn will also have difficulties holding the Parliamentary Labour Party (PLP) together and it may well prove beyond him. However much he may try to use his huge mandate to persuade Labour MPs to follow him, he cannot avoid the reality that most of them do not share many of his more extreme beliefs. We may see the end of the Labour Party as we have known it. We may also see a period of disunity within Labour resulting in a crushing electoral defeat in 2020. On the other hand, it is just possible that Corbyn has tuned into a new mood in the country which is a reaction against the policies of both Labour and the Conservatives in recent years. In order to convert this into electoral victory in 2020 he will have to bring millions of people who have previously been inactive, into the process. It will also be interesting and important to see how well he can make inroads into SNP support in Scotland.

Exam focus

To consolidate your knowledge of this chapter, answer the following questions:

1 To what extent is Labour now a divided party?
2 How democratic was the election of Jeremy Corbyn as Labour Party leader?
3 To what extent is Labour now 'unelectable?'
4 To what extent do the ideas of Jeremy Corbyn and his supporters conform to traditional socialist principles?
5 To what extent do the ideas of Jeremy Corbyn and his supporters depart from the policies of 'New Labour?'
6 Has Jeremy Corbyn ushered in 'a new kind of politics'?

Chapter 2

The 2015 general election: a new era of Conservative domination?

Exam success

The up-to-date facts, examples and arguments in this chapter will help you to produce good quality answers in your AS unit tests in the following areas of the specification:

Edexcel	AQA	OCR
Unit 1	**Unit 1**	**Unit F851**
Elections	Electoral systems	Elections and referenda
Party policies and ideas	Political parties	Political parties

Context

What purposes do general elections serve? This apparently simple question is actually more complex than it at first seems. It is important to remind ourselves of these functions in order to place the result in context.

The purposes of a general election and their implications include:

- To ensure that each constituency has an MP who can represent its interests and those of the constituents individually where necessary. In this sense the overall result is not relevant as each MP should represent the constituency without favouring those who may have voted for him or her; nor should it matter whether the MP represents the governing party or any other.
- To elect a government. Here the 2015 election was rather more successful than its predecessor in 2010 — 2010 did not produce a clear result but 2015 did, with the Conservative Party winning an overall majority of 12 in the House of Commons.
- To give the new government a mandate. This mandate is based on the winning party's manifesto. Here again 2010 was a failure as the electorate did not know in advance what the agreed coalition policies would be. Indeed they did not know whether a coalition would be formed or which parties would take part. Therefore there was no electoral mandate for the 2010–15 coalition government. This called into question some of its *legitimacy*. After 2015 all this has changed. Having won according to the constitutional rules governing the first-past-the-post electoral system (by winning an overall majority of the seats in the House of Commons, at least 326), the Conservative government has a mandate to implement its manifesto commitments. It is, in other words, fully *legitimate*.

- To give the electorate an opportunity to force the outgoing government to *account* for its policies — to publicise its successes and to accept or counter criticism of its failures. This was a problem in the 2015 election as it was not clear to the electorate which of the two coalition parties was responsible for which policies. For example, the Conservatives tried to claim the high ground where economic policy was concerned, while the Liberal Democrats claimed responsibility for tax cuts for low earners. The Liberal Democrats also claimed that the welfare cuts which were made would have been more severe had they not restrained the Conservatives. So the electorate had a tough task in deciding who was responsible for what. The result, in which the Conservatives gained ground while the Liberal Democrats were all but wiped out, suggests that much of the electorate decided to give credit to the Conservatives for some successes while punishing the Liberal Democrats for unpopular policies, notably the large rise in university tuition fees. Nevertheless, this election demonstrated how difficult it can be to call government to account when more than one party is involved. The position will be much clearer in 2020.
- To offer a choice to the electorate, between parties, between potential teams of ministers and between potential prime ministers. Arguably the 2015 election offered a more realistic choice to the electorate than ever. As well as the three main parties, there was wide choice in Scotland and Wales, with the nationalists to the fore, UKIP made a strong showing and the Green Party was more prominent than in the past. As for potential prime ministers, the choice between David Cameron and Ed Miliband was of special importance, notably because Miliband had such a poor media image and because the Conservatives chose to target him as one of Labour's main weaknesses. Indeed many commentators have argued that, with a different leader, notably David Miliband, Labour might have won the election. But the electorate were not offered that choice.
- To help educate the public by airing the great political issues of the day. In this sense the election was also a success. Key issues such as welfare reform, how to deal with the budget deficit, what to do about immigration, whether there should be a referendum on UK membership of the EU and whether to renew the UK's nuclear weapons capability were hotly debated. Nobody who chose to make themselves informed could complain that they were not aware of where the parties and individual politicians stood on such issues.

How significant was the Conservative victory?

Before considering this it is important to review the overall result. This is shown in Table 2.1.

Table 2.1 The UK general election, 7 May 2015

Party	Seats won	% seats	Change in seats since 2010	% votes	% change in votes since 2010
Conservative	331	51.0	+24	36.9	+0.8
Labour	232	35.7	−26	30.4	+1.5
SNP*	56	8.6	+50	4.7*	+3.1
Liberal Democrat	8	1.2	−49	7.9	−15.2
Democratic Unionist* (NI)	8	1.2	0	0.6*	0.0
Sinn Fein* (NI)	4	0.6	−1	0.6*	0.0
Plaid Cymru*	3	0.5	0	0.6*	0.0
SDLP* (NI)	3	0.5	0	0.3*	0.0
Ulster Unionist* (NI)	2	0.3	+2	0.4*	0.0
UKIP	1	0.2	+1	12.6	+9.5
Green Party	1	0.2	0	3.8	+2.8
Others	1	0.0	−1	1.2	−2.5
Total	**650**				

*These parties only put up candidates in their own countries, not in the UK as a whole, so their percentage share appears lower than it was in those countries. For example, the SNP won 50% of the votes in Scotland but only 4.7% of total UK votes

Turnout: 66.1%

A good result for the Conservatives…

This was a good result for the Conservative Party in these senses:

- The party won an overall majority and so could form a government alone without the constraints which would be imposed by a coalition partner.
- For most of the campaign the parties were apparently neck and neck in the polls, but a late surge gave victory to the Conservatives, suggesting they ran a very successful campaign.
- Labour, the main rival, was soundly beaten. The Conservative Party ended up with 99 more seats than Labour.
- The Conservatives increased their share of the national vote by 0.8%, represented by an increase in their popular vote of 630,922.
- The Liberal Democrats lost all but eight of their seats, suggesting that the electorate blamed them for some of the failures of the coalition, rather than blaming the Conservatives. The Conservatives won all 15 seats previously held by the Liberal Democrats in southwest England.
- Labour was left in disarray by its defeat and so will have problems mounting a successful opposition or challenging for power in 2020, not least because of a highly disruptive leadership election and its aftermath.

- The Conservatives successfully fought off the challenge of UKIP, restricting it to just one seat in Clacton.
- As Table 2.2 shows, the Conservatives won a huge majority, of 105, over all other parties if we consider English constituencies alone. This will mean that, where there are House of Commons votes on English-only issues, if the nationalist parties withdraw as is likely in the future (under the system of English Votes for English Laws, or EVEL), the Conservative Party will enjoy a comfortable majority.
- David Cameron received a major boost to his own standing. This will give him not only enhanced power over his own party but also greater authority in his dealings with foreign powers and with the European Union.

Table 2.2 The 2015 general election in England alone

Party	Seats won	% seats won	Change in seats won since 2010	% vote	Change in % vote since 2010
Conservative	319	59.8	+21	41.0	+1.4
Labour	206	38.6	+16	31.6	+3.5
Liberal Democrat	6	1.1	−37	8.2	−16.0
UKIP	1	0.1	+1	14.1	+10.6
Green Party	1	0.1	0	4.2	+3.2
Others	0	0.0	−1	2.7*	+0.9

*Some figures have been rounded up or down

Turnout 65.9%

...or a disappointing result for the Conservatives?

However, this was a disappointing result for the Conservative Party in these senses:

- The party's overall House of Commons majority is only 12. This makes the government vulnerable to backbench revolts, which may well occur over such issues as the terms and timing of the EU referendum, the introduction of a British Bill of Rights and some welfare and tax reforms. Already, the government has had to abandon proposed parliamentary votes on fox hunting and Sunday trading laws because it feared it could not command a Commons majority.
- Despite the party's 'victory', it actually made little headway in terms of the overall popular vote. It won because it was able to convert a modest increase in its popular vote (of 0.8%) into an additional 24 seats to gain its majority. This was not a ringing endorsement from the electorate.
- The party only won 36.9% of the popular vote. Given there was a turnout of 66%, this meant that only 24% of those *eligible* to vote actually voted Conservative. To put this in context, the party won 36.1% of the vote in 2010 and Labour only won 35.2% in 2001, so this is part of a long-term trend.

- The Conservatives have little representation in Scotland (one seat) and Wales (eleven seats). In Scotland especially, therefore, this calls into question the legitimacy of the government. The result of this 'legitimacy gap' has already led to loud renewed calls for extensive devolution and possibly another referendum on full Scottish independence.

So the position is balanced. However, overall, given the circumstances and the unpromising prospects this was an excellent result for the Conservatives.

What are the prospects for the Conservatives?

There is much evidence to suggest that the prospects are good for the party. In particular it is the state of the UK economy that may well be crucial. It is a common belief in politics that economic policy is crucial in determining which party people support. Early research suggests that more of the electorate trusted the Conservatives on the economy than trusted Labour. In addition, a number of economic indicators remain positive. Economic growth is higher than in the rest of Europe, the government deficit is falling, unemployment remains low, wages are rising after a long period of stagnation, and inflation and interest rates are very low. If this continues the Conservative government will reap the benefits. Many experts believe that these improvements will last for several years to come.

However, a number of other structural factors favour the Conservatives. Among them are:
- The centre-left of UK politics is now fragmented. Five parties are proposing left-of centre policies. These are Labour, the Liberal Democrats, the Scottish National Party, Plaid Cymru in Wales and the Green Party. The centre-right, however, is represented by one party — the Conservatives. UKIP, with its right-wing ideas, could damage the Conservatives but this did not happen in the 2015 election, mainly because the UKIP vote was dispersed too widely. The UK electoral system hugely favours parties that concentrate support and discriminates against those with dispersed or fragmented support, so the centre-left has a huge disadvantage, as does UKIP.
- The rise of the SNP in Scotland, which now seems to be secure for some time to come, means that the Labour Party will find it extremely difficult to gain an overall majority in the House of Commons in the future.
- The Labour Party now appears too internally divided to be able to mount a successful challenge or to provide a sustainable opposition in Parliament.
- The Liberal Democrats, having been decimated in the election, are also no longer able to make a serious challenge.
- Tony Blair, among others, has asserted that the party that hopes to win power must capture the centre ground. In 2015 the Conservatives appear to have achieved that. Their policies were very much aimed at those on middle incomes and those who hold moderate political views. These groups form the majority of the electorate.

Summary

It is now difficult to see how the Conservative Party could be dislodged from power in 2020. Most of the signs are in its favour. What can prevent a long period of Conservative domination? The following table provides a risk assessment for the Conservatives:

Nature of risk	Likelihood	Likely consequences
A general economic decline in the UK	Relatively small	Could result in electoral defeat
A foreign policy negative issue such as the 2003 Iraq War	Could happen in relation to Syria	The Conservative government could survive this
Internal divisions within the Conservative Party	Could happen over the EU referendum and its consequences	Possibility of parliamentary defeats could shorten the life of the government
The Labour Party could mount a credible challenge	As things stand in 2015 this looks very unlikely	The electoral arithmetic suggests even a resurgent Labour Party would have difficulty overhauling the Conservatives
Reform of the electoral system would make outright victory impossible at the next election	Highly unlikely	A complete transformation in the party system resulting in coalition governments in the future

The evidence suggests that a prolonged period of Conservative government is more likely than not. Recent history is also on the Conservatives' side. Since 1951 we have seen four periods of domination by one or the other of the main parties:

- 1951–64: Conservative governments only
- 1964–79: Labour governments interrupted only by 4 years of a Conservative administration
- 1979–97: Conservative governments only
- 1997–2010: Labour governments only

It seems that once a party gains power it tends to hang on to it for a long time.

Exam focus

To consolidate your knowledge of this chapter, answer the following questions:

1 Discuss the influence of 'small' parties in UK politics.
2 For what reasons did the Conservatives win the 2015 general election?
3 Why did Labour lose the 2015 general election?
4 How did the 2015 general election affect the party system in the UK?

The 2015 general election: the constitutional implications

Exam success

The up-to-date facts, examples and arguments in this chapter will help you to produce good quality answers in your AS unit tests in the following areas of the specification:

Edexcel	AQA	OCR
Unit 1	**Unit 1**	**Unit F851**
Elections	Electoral systems	Electoral systems and referenda
Unit2	**Unit 2**	**Unit F852**
The UK constitution	Multi-level governance	The constitution
	The British constitution	

Context

The outcome of the 2015 election has thrown up a number of interesting constitutional questions. Of course, had there been another hung parliament, that would have created its own problems, especially if the SNP had held the balance of power, but that did not happen. Nevertheless, some key issues are brought into focus by the result. There are four potential questions:

- The first concerns the future of the first-past-the-post electoral system.
- The second concerns the implications of the SNP totally dominating its own country.
- Third, there is the issue of what happens in the House of Commons when there is no coherent opposition.
- Finally, and this is linked to the third question, there is the issue of what should be done about the House of Lords.

The first-past-the-post electoral system

Apart from the fact that the Conservative Party gained an overall majority against apparently great odds, the most striking feature of the election was the way in which the first-past-the-post (FPTP) electoral system affected the results, in particular the extremely uneven way in which votes were converted into seats.

The key examples of this phenomenon are:

- The Scottish National Party won almost exactly 50% of the popular vote in Scotland, but gained over 90% of the seats. It was indeed a triumph for the SNP, but its success was hugely exaggerated.
- The national share of the vote gained by the Liberal Democrats fell markedly. The party lost about two-thirds of its popular support, down from 23.1% to 7.9%. However, this resulted in its losing most of its seats, down from 57 to 8.
- UKIP achieved a major success by gaining 12.6% of the national vote from a very low base in 2010, but this was only converted into one solitary seat (Clacton, won by Douglas Carswell, who already held the seat from an earlier by-election). If we look at England alone, the discrepancy is even more striking as UKIP won 14.1% of the English popular vote.
- The Green Party gained 3.8% of the national vote (4.2% in England) but only managed to retain one seat in Brighton.
- The so-called 'winner's bonus' operated dramatically. The Conservatives gained 51% of the seats available from a popular vote of 36.9%. This enabled it to form a majority government. The reason was that the party concentrated its support in southern England where it won the vast majority of the seats and where much of the population is concentrated. Interestingly, Labour did not enjoy such an advantage in the way that it has done in the past. It won 35.7% of the seats from 30.4% of the national votes — not far off a proportional outcome.

All these effects are striking. However, perhaps the most interesting statistic concerns the different value of votes. In theory British democracy grants one vote per adult, making everyone equal within the electoral system. The reality of how the votes translate into seats, however, is very different.

If we take the *total* number of votes won by each party and divide it by the number of seats each of those parties won, we obtain a figure which is the *average* number of votes needed to elect each MP from that party. Table 3.1 illustrates this.

These statistics demonstrate clearly how much more valuable a vote for the SNP was, compared to a vote for UKIP. It also shows the advantage for Conservative voters over Labour voters.

We can put this effect in another way — a large number of votes are wasted under FPTP. Wasted votes are those that cannot affect the outcome either in an individual constituency or in the country as a whole. 'Wasted' votes include:

- votes in 'safe' seats where only one party can conceivably win
- votes for small parties that will make no significant impact
- votes for parties, such as UKIP and the Liberal Democrats, whose support is so dispersed that they cannot win many seats

Table 3.1 Average votes needed to gain each party a seat in 2015

SNP (figures only relate to votes and seats in Scotland)	
Total votes	1,454,436
Total seats	56
Average votes per seat won	**25,972**
Conservative	
Total votes	11,334,576
Total seats	330
Average votes per seat won	**34,347**
Labour	
Total votes	9,347,304
Total seats	232
Average votes per seat won	**40,290**
UKIP	
Total votes	3,881,099
Total seats	1
Average votes per seat won	**3,881,099**

Conversely, some votes are much more valuable. These are:

■ votes in close, marginal constituencies where 'every vote counts'
■ votes for parties, such as the SNP, whose impact is exaggerated by the electoral system

All of these phenomena were evident in the 2015 election, perhaps more so than ever before. The **Electoral Reform Society**, which campaigns for a change to the electoral system, described the 2015 general election as:

> the nail in the coffin for our voting system. FPTP was designed for a time when nearly everyone voted for one of the two biggest parties. But people have changed and our system cannot cope...The Conservatives have won a majority in parliament on not much more than a third of the vote. So, while the prospect of a hung parliament has receded, the problems with our voting system have remained in the foreground.
>
> Source: reported in *Guardian,* 9 May 2015

Supporters of the electoral system argue that, though such criticisms may be valid, they are more than compensated for by the electoral system's ability to convert a fragmented party system into a single-party majority government, something which proportional systems rarely do. In addition, the main beneficiaries of the system, the Conservative Party, have no intention of placing electoral reform on the agenda. So, although it may be said there is a 'legitimacy issue' in UK electoral politics, this is not yet a constitutional crisis and is unlikely to be resolved any time soon.

SNP dominance in Scotland

Two problems arise here — **English Votes for English Laws (EVEL)** and the continuing issue of **devolution** and possible future **full independence**:

EVEL

Had the SNP held the balance of power after the election, i.e. neither main party could have commanded a majority without its support, there would have been a huge constitutional issue over Scotland. The Scottish nationalists would have placed their demands at the top of their agenda. It is even probable that the granting of extensive autonomy to Scotland, perhaps even a new referendum on full independence, would have been the 'price to be paid' for their support. But this did not happen. Nevertheless, the SNP's dominant showing in Scotland has created something of a constitutional crisis and David Cameron has admitted as much. He knows that the SNP is demanding full fiscal autonomy (i.e. full control by the devolved Scottish government over the taxes it collects and how it spends them) and that if he does not grant it (which he is reluctant to do), support for the SNP may continue to grow.

However, the main issue now concerns EVEL — English Votes for English Laws. With such a large group of SNP MPs in the Commons, the government runs the danger of losing votes if it cannot rely on the full support of all its own MPs. With a slender Commons majority of 12, such possibilities may become quite common. The first skirmish has already taken place. In November the SNP effectively blocked a proposal to relax the Sunday trading laws, although these apply only to England. The SNP proved to be so determined that the government dropped the proposal. Leading Conservatives were furious. Why, they argued, should SNP MPs be able to influence hunting laws in England, while English MPs have no say at all over hunting laws in Scotland (it is controlled by the Scottish Parliament)?

The government response was to introduce a proposal in November whereby, on English-only issues (to be determined by the Commons Speaker), all MPs will be allowed to debate and vote, but the English MPs (an English 'grand committee') would have a final veto.

Devolution and independence for Scotland

EVEL is not the only constitutional issue that needs settlement as soon as possible. The SNP gains have put the party in a strong position to negotiate considerable transfers of powers from Westminster to Scotland. It has already been agreed that control over income tax rates can be devolved and that the Scottish government will have control over half the VAT (Value Added Tax) receipts collected in Scotland, but the SNP wants more and claims that the election result in Scotland gives it a mandate to demand more.

Further down the line comes the issue of whether the Scots should have an early opportunity to vote again on the issue of full independence. The SNP argues that, as for greater devolution, its election success suggests there is growing support for more independence. Furthermore, the SNP has argued that the 'No' vote on independence was obtained on the basis of promises by English parties that there would be extensive devolution of powers, but that these promises are not being met. In other words, the 'No' vote was won on false premises. If the SNP achieves a similar success in the elections to the Scottish Parliament in May 2016, there will be renewed pressure to hold a fresh referendum. If the outcome of the negotiations on devolution during 2015–16 proves to be unsatisfactory for the Scots, a new threat to the United Kingdom may emerge.

No coherent opposition

The UK constitution acknowledges the existence of a coherent, identifiable 'Her Majesty's opposition'. It is called 'Her Majesty's' because it is recognised in many of the procedures of Parliament and the state in general. The leader of the opposition is an official position, carrying a large salary and the privilege of taking part in official state occasions. Above all, however, it is in Parliament that opposition is most significant.

In particular, part of the parliamentary agenda is given over to the opposition for them to decide what issues should be debated. At Prime Minister's Question Time the leader of the opposition is given the spotlight in calling the prime minister to account. Above all, however, it is the role of the opposition to call government in general to account and to offer an alternative set of policies. This is seen as a vital aspect of UK democracy.

Normally the 'opposition' and its leader are well defined. It is the party that has the second largest representation in Parliament and the leader of the opposition is the recognised leader of that party. Though he or she does not have the same status, even the leader of the third party takes an official role on state occasions. But following the 2015 election the UK has a fragmented opposition. The Labour Party is divided between those who support its elected leader and those who do not. There are 56 Scottish MPs in Parliament too, all of whom are ultimately committed to taking Scotland out of the UK. With such a fragmented opposition the old characteristic of 'opposition versus government', on which much parliamentary procedure and practice is based, has been removed.

This will be a challenge to the flexible UK constitution, which is normally able to adapt to changing circumstances. It will also be a challenge to the speaker, John Bercow, whose responsibility it will be to solve this new puzzle.

The House of Lords: what should be done?

Why should an election to the House of Commons affect the role of the House of Lords? At first one might think there is no connection, but this may not be the case. The answer lies, to some extent, in the problem of opposition described above. If we are entering a period of ineffective opposition in the House of Commons, as many commentators fear, the House of Lords may well become increasingly significant in calling government to account. Yet, at this crucial time, the House of Lords has been brought into disrepute. There are three particular problems:

- The size of the Lords is growing and may now be doing so at a faster rate than before. In August 2015 a further 45 peers were created, bringing the size of the house up to 820. Apart from the fact that life expectancy is increasing, so peers are serving for longer, each new government has been taking the opportunity to appoint new peers who will support it. It also opens it to fresh charges that it is merely a reflection of 'political patronage' and is losing its independence: 186 new life peers were appointed during 2010–15, compared to only 34 in Gordon Brown's government of 2007–10. In July 2015 there were 820 peers compared to 666 in 1999. It has, critics say, become too large and unwieldy and has therefore lost focus on its important roles.

- After a number of scandals concerning the conduct of serving peers, in particular over their claims for expenses and their connections with dubious business interests, often abroad, July 2015 saw probably the worst scandal when Lord Sewel was caught in a newspaper 'sting' consorting with prostitutes, using cocaine and openly criticising senior politicians from all parties. Though Sewel resigned, the Lords has weak procedures for controlling the conduct of peers and cannot remove their peerages. The real issue that such incidents illustrate is that the peers, being not elected, are not accountable. Calls for an elected second chamber are likely to increase following the Sewel affair.

- The Lords is once again constrained by the 'Salisbury Convention'. Now that the government has won a majority, the Salisbury Convention demands that the Lords must not obstruct any measures that were commitments in the governing party's last election manifesto. When there was a coalition the convention was suspended, making the Lords more independent and therefore more effective. The House of Lords' forcing a delay on the implementation of cuts to tax credits in November brought this problem into focus, precipitating an inquiry into the powers of the house, led by Lord Strathclyde.

Summary

The next 5 years are likely to see a succession of constitutional issues coming to the fore. Among them will be:

- British membership of the EU
- the possible replacement of the European Convention on Human Rights by a British Bill of Rights
- further devolution to Scotland, Wales and Northern Ireland
- devolution of powers to several English cities
- new demands for a second referendum on Scottish independence

Yet following the general election there are serious questions about how effective Parliament can be in the face of these crucial debates, given the small government majority, its dubious legitimacy, the fragmentation of opposition, the existence of a dissident group of Scottish MPs and the vagaries of the first-past-the-post electoral system.

Exam focus

To consolidate your knowledge of this chapter, answer the following questions:

1 How did the 2015 general election demonstrate the impact of the first-past-the-post electoral system?
2 Explain the nature and role of the 'opposition' in parliamentary politics.
3 Examine the case for saying that the UK government is no longer legitimate in Scotland.
4 Critically assess the solutions that have been proposed to the 'English Question'.
5 Is the House of Lords now the only effective opposition to government?

Chapter 4

Devolution: is a federal UK inevitable?

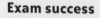

Exam success

The up-to-date facts, examples and arguments in this chapter will help you to produce good quality answers in your AS unit tests in the following areas of the specification:

Edexcel	AQA	OCR
Unit 2	**Unit 2**	**Unit F852**
The constitution	Multi-level governance	The constitution

Context

This question can only be discussed if we have a firm idea of what the term 'federal' actually means in constitutional terms. In general terms, a federal system has the following characteristics:

- Sovereignty, i.e. ultimate political authority, is divided between a central authority, normally known as the 'federal government', and regional authorities which go by various names such as **states** (USA, Australia, India), **Länder** (Germany), **provinces** (Canada) or **federal subjects** (Russia).
- The fact that sovereignty is so divided means that there must be a supreme federal constitution. Such a constitution establishes and describes the division of sovereignty, asserting which sovereign powers are reserved to the central authorities, and which are reserved to the regional authorities.
- A federal constitution must be **entrenched**. This means the division of powers is safeguarded and cannot be changed without a constitutional amendment. The devices for such constitutional amendments usually contain safeguards to protect the interests of the federal regions, so that their powers are not simply absorbed by the central authority over time.
- The division of sovereignty is **symmetric**. This means that each sovereign regional authority has powers which are equal to those enjoyed by all the others.
- The central authority may only take over the powers reserved to regional authorities in some kind of emergency situation (usually called **emergency powers**) such as war or major public disorder.
- The main variation between one federal system and another concerns powers not specified in the constitution. For example, in the USA, any powers *not* mentioned in the constitution are automatically reserved to the 50 states (the forces of decentralisation are very powerful in the USA). In other systems, such as Russia, any such powers are automatically claimed by the central authority.

The UK fails to meet all these criteria. There is no entrenched constitution, the powers granted to national regions are asymmetric (for example, Scotland has more powers than Wales and Northern Ireland) and all legal sovereignty lies with the central authority — the Westminster Parliament.

After 2010/11 a new force questioned this apparently fixed set of circumstances — this was the rise of the Scottish National Party (SNP). The SNP won the 2011 election to the Scottish Parliament with an overall majority. It immediately began to demand a referendum on full independence. This was defeated by 55–45%, but it was clear that there was a new mood for greater autonomy in the country. When the SNP won nearly all the Scottish seats in the 2015 general election the whole issue of devolution and independence was renewed. Nevertheless, the reality of parliamentary sovereignty seemed to be an insurmountable obstacle.

Is the UK heading for federalism?

Given this situation it seems a strange question to ask whether the UK is now *effectively* a federal system or whether it will become federal in the future. The reasons it is being asked are twofold:

- A great deal of power (not sovereignty) has been delegated to the national regions in the form of **devolution**. Although the division of these powers is not entrenched, it could be said that it is so unlikely that they would ever be returned to Westminster that it might as well be described as federalism. To underpin this idea, it has to be remembered that the devolution settlements of 1997–98 were approved by referendums in Scotland, Wales and Northern Ireland. It could be argued that a referendum effectively does entrench the division of powers.
- The results of recent elections to the Scottish Parliament and of the 2015 general election, when the Scottish National Party won nearly all the Scottish constituencies, suggest there is now an irresistible drive towards national autonomy. If Scotland is granted more autonomy, there is a likelihood that Wales and Northern Ireland will soon follow suit. Indeed it has also been argued that, if the UK does not become a federal system, Scotland at least will simply vote for full independence in the future.

Of course this is speculation. It may also be that, by granting more powers (stopping short of actual sovereignty) to Scotland, Wales and Northern Ireland, the desire for greater national autonomy will be satisfied and the UK will not move towards federalism.

The existing devolution settlement

The status of devolution is as follows:

- The powers which have been transferred from the central government and Parliament to devolved executives and assemblies have only been **delegated**. This implies that they can be taken back by simple parliamentary statute at

Westminster. In the past, for example, the powers granted to Northern Ireland have been reclaimed by central government as a result of widespread public disorder there. This was known as **direct rule**.

- Where there is a dispute over whether certain powers have indeed been devolved (i.e. the devolution acts are unclear or circumstances have changed), the UK judiciary will decide where such powers reside.
- As we have seen above, it is **asymmetric**. Different degrees of power have been granted to Scotland (the most), Northern Ireland and Wales (the least).
- The Westminster Parliament remains sovereign. All the devolution arrangements could be cancelled by a simple statute. This also means that the devolved administrations cannot claim powers which are not contained in the devolution legislation.

Scottish demands for 'federalism'

Table 4.1 shows the current state of the Scottish devolution debate. It lists the current devolution settlement, the current proposals from the government due to be implemented in 2016 and finally the key demands for further devolution being promoted by the SNP.

Table 4.1 The Scottish devolution debate

	The current settlement	The changes proposed by government	What the SNP is demanding*
Europe	It will be the decision of the people of the UK as a whole whether the UK remains a member of the EU	No change	A 'double lock' would be put on a referendum. The UK could only leave the EU if Scotland, Wales and Northern Ireland all voted for leaving
Income tax	Scotland can only vary the rate of income tax by 3%	Scotland will have control over rates of income tax and will keep all income tax collected in Scotland	No change
VAT	Scotland has no control over the rate of VAT and Scotland does not control the revenue from VAT raised in Scotland	Scotland will not control the VAT rate and will keep half the proceeds of VAT raised in Scotland	Scotland will retain control of all the proceeds of VAT raised in Scotland
National Insurance	Scotland has no control over NI rates and has no access to the proceeds	No change	Scotland will control NI rates and retain the proceeds raised in Scotland

Table 4.1 The Scottish devolution debate (Continued)

	The current settlement	The changes proposed by government	What the SNP is demanding*
Other taxes	Scotland has no control over other taxes	Scotland to have control over Air Passenger Duty but virtually no other taxes	Scotland to have control over virtually all taxes, including corporate taxes, inheritance tax, capital gains tax, petroleum revenue tax and stamp duty, and will retain all the proceeds for use in Scotland
Fiscal policy	Scotland has no control over overall government finances including borrowing	The Scottish government should have the power to borrow funds for capital investment only	Scotland to have borrowing powers for both capital and other forms of spending if required, so that its financial position may be different from that of the UK as a whole
Minimum wage	Scotland has no control over the living wage level	No change	Scotland to have control over setting the living wage in its own country
Welfare benefit rates	Scotland has no control over benefit rates	Scotland will have very limited control over most benefit rates	Scotland will have extensive control over many benefit rates
Voting	The voting age is the same (18) throughout the UK	Scotland may vary the voting age for elections to its own parliament and local government	As the government's proposal
Defence	Scotland should have no control over defence policy	No change	Scotland to have the right to remove nuclear weapons from its territory

*Subject to change

The SNP has said that it wants to see the same powers devolved as are reserved to the German *Länder* (provinces). In other words, it uses the German federal system as the model for its demands. Should they be met, therefore, devolution would constitute 'quasi-federalism'.

Wales

The **Wales Act**, passed in December 2014, detailed proposals for further devolution to Wales. Its main proposals are:

- The Welsh Assembly will have the right to set a new voting age for elections to its assembly and for local government.
- Wales will be given the power to hold a referendum on whether the country should have control over some of its income tax rates and revenue.
- Wales will be be able to set the rates of some other taxes, including stamp duty (tax on house purchases), business rates and landfill tax.
- The Assembly will be granted new powers over such issues as fracking and wind farms, public transport and sewerage.
- The Assembly will be able to change its name to a 'parliament' if it wishes. This would reflect its change into a proper legislature after 2011.
- The possibility is opened up that Wales would be granted additional, though very limited powers, over some legislation.

Though Wales has been granted additional devolved powers in recent years, they are still very limited, much more so than in Scotland. Thus the description 'quasi-federalism' would be a gross exaggeration. The Welsh people are also unlikely to want any significant increase in powers for the Welsh Assembly.

Northern Ireland

Northern Ireland was granted more devolved powers than Wales in 1998, but much less power than Scotland. The Northern Ireland assembly has the following powers:

- over most laws applying in the province
- policing and security
- healthcare
- social services
- social security payments
- education
- transport
- local government and housing

Whether there will be further devolution to Northern Ireland remains uncertain. The unionist parties are reluctant to see such a development, but Sinn Fein would like more autonomous powers to be transferred (its ultimate aim is full independence from the UK, like the SNP in Scotland, and the unification of Ireland).

English regions

Chapter 7 of this update describes the proposals for a new 'Northern Hub' involving increased powers for English city regions. The change would include the introduction of elected mayors and enhanced borrowing powers for the new regions. However, this would be a far cry from anything that looks like federalism. English cities have never shown any great desire for more autonomy (several, for example, recently rejected the opportunity to introduce elected mayors). The kind of powers being suggested by George Osborne would be modest, mainly amounting to increased control over the cities' existing share of revenue, together with greater borrowing powers.

Summary

If we ask the question of whether federalism is inevitable in the UK, the answer must be no. The reasons for this are:

- A federal system would mean the end of parliamentary sovereignty. It seems unlikely that Parliament would ever surrender this position.
- Federalism would require the creation of a codified constitution which would be entrenched and stand above parliamentary sovereignty. Though this is a popular proposal among politicians of a liberal disposition, the political will for such a change may not be strong enough for a long time to come.
- There is a relatively weak appetite for federalism in Wales and Northern Ireland and among the English regions.
- Should a federal settlement *only* involve Scotland's relations with the rest of the UK, it would be extremely unbalanced.
- Only the Liberal Democrats and the SNP seriously support the idea of federalism.

If, on the other hand, we change the question to whether a 'quasi-federal' system is inevitable, the answer is less certain. Whether Scotland can achieve significantly more devolved powers than are currently proposed will depend largely on the future fortunes of the SNP. In May 2016 there will be new elections to the Scottish Parliament. Should the SNP increase its existing majority substantially, there would be extreme pressure on the UK government to grant SNP demands. Prospects for a similar development in Wales or Northern Ireland look more remote.

Exam focus

To consolidate your knowledge of this chapter, answer the following questions:

1 What are the main features of a federal political system?
2 How does devolution differ from federalism?
3 Why are there currently so many demands for further devolution?
4 Why are there increasing demands for a new federal settlement in the UK?
5 What is meant by the term 'quasi-federalism'?

Chapter 5

The EU referendum: a defining moment in UK politics?

Context

The last time there was a referendum on the UK's membership of the European Union was in 1975. The context was not totally unlike today:

- Then, as now, the governing party (Labour in 1975) was split on whether the UK should remain in the European Community.
- Then, as is proposed now, the government had renegotiated the terms of UK membership.
- Then, also, public opinion seemed to be fairly equally divided in advance of the referendum campaign.

At the start of the 1975 campaign it seemed that a 'No' (i.e. 'leave') vote was quite likely, but by the end the result was decisive:

	No. of votes	%
For staying in the European Community	17,378,581	67.23
For leaving the European Community	8,470,073	32.77

Turnout: 65%

Although there were claims that the 'Yes' campaign had more resources available to it, the decisiveness of the result silenced the referendum's critics.

During the coalition government of 2010–15 the Conservative Party developed the idea that, if elected to government in 2015, ministers would attempt to renegotiate the terms of UK membership and persuade its European partners to develop internal reforms of the EU. The party made a manifesto commitment to hold a referendum on the issue by 2017.

There will be a problem if David Cameron and George Osborne fail to get any meaningful concessions from the rest of the EU. Will they admit defeat and join the 'No to Europe' campaign or will they accept the unsatisfactory nature of the UK's membership? It will certainly be difficult for them to campaign for the UK to stay in an unsatisfactory organisation.

Why is UK membership such a key issue?

There are a number of reasons why the new Conservative government believes a referendum is essential:

- It is 40 years since the last EU referendum and there are many who argue it is time for another vote on the issue. There are now two generations who have not been given the opportunity to give their opinion.
- Immigration has become a major issue in British politics. However, it is a basic principle of the EU that there should be free movement of people and labour. This means that, as a full member, the UK cannot close its borders to migrants from EU countries. Furthermore, the rules of the EU do not allow the UK to discriminate (mainly in terms of available welfare benefits) against such migrants in order to deter them from entering the country.
- The rise of UKIP has forced the Conservative Party to address the issue. UKIP is opposed to UK membership and attracted 12.6% of the national vote in 2015.
- There is a significant minority of the Conservative Party (possibly 60–100 MPs) who are eurosceptics and either oppose UK membership altogether or demand deep reforms to the way the EU works. This minority may well cause problems for the party leadership. It should also be emphasised that there are members of the current cabinet who are eurosceptics, so the long-term unity of the government is also at stake.
- There is a widespread and long-held belief that the European Union is fundamentally internally undemocratic, in particular that its decision-making processes are not accountable enough. The main critics suggest that the UK has given up too much sovereignty to Europe and that some of this needs to be reclaimed.

The arguments for and against UK membership

Table 5.1 compares the arguments for the UK remaining within the EU against those in favour of departure.

Table 5.1 Arguments concerning UK membership of the EU

In favour of membership	Against membership
Most economists, though not all, argue that there are enormous benefits to the British economy from membership. This is the result of free trade and the access it gives UK firms to a huge European market	Membership takes away flexibility for UK economic policy, notably over corporation taxes, wage levels, working practices and consumer protection measures
Being a member increases the UK's influence in the world by being part of such a powerful political and economic bloc	The UK loses some independence over its own foreign policy positions
The free movement of people and labour gives UK citizens the right to work and live in large parts of Europe	The UK is unable to control its borders effectively because of free movement of people within the EU. This has become especially acute since the migrant crisis worsened dramatically during the summer of 2015
The EU features pooled sovereignty. Therefore, although the UK has lost some national sovereignty it also now has some influence over affairs in other EU states	Many decisions are now made outside the UK, in the European Commission and Council of Ministers. Therefore the UK has lost a great deal of sovereignty
Trade unions in particular argue that the EU guarantees rights for workers which would be in jeopardy if we withdrew. Consumer groups believe that consumer protection is best guaranteed within the EU	There is excessive 'red tape' in the EU, which holds back economic growth
Some parts of the UK would suffer from the loss of EU grants and subsidies, notably agriculture and areas of deprivation such as deprived inner cities and areas of high unemployment	The UK is a net contributor to EU funds, i.e. it pays more to the EU than it receives in various subsidies and grants. It can be argued that the UK would receive a boost to public finances if it left
British membership will prevent the complete domination of Europe by a two-state axis — Germany and France	Eurosceptics argue that it will be possible for the UK to remain in a customs union, i.e. without tariffs on imports and exports, and so retain the economic benefits, but not be part of a political union

The political consequences of leaving

No attempt will be made here to assess the economic impact of the UK leaving the EU, not least because economists themselves disagree on the issue. This assessment will concentrate on the political outcomes.

If the UK leaves the European Union, the political consequences will be far reaching. The likely possibilities include:

- A large amount of legislation will have to be passed in order to replace current EU legislation. Parliament might be busy with the task for several years and many issues, such as workplace rights, consumer protection, and agricultural and industrial subsidies, will be fought over between the parties.
- The SNP has pointed out that, if Scotland votes to stay in the EU, while the UK as a whole votes to leave, there will be a constitutional crisis and the demands for full Scottish independence might well become irresistible. To a lesser extent the same problem applies to Wales.
- It will probably end the great schism in the Conservative Party between pro and anti-European factions. This will be a comfort to the party, which constantly threatens to fall apart over Europe.
- It may well be that UKIP will go out of existence. Its principal raison d'être will no longer exist, so the appeal of the party will become limited (Box 5.1).
- There will be a great debate over how best to manage immigration with the constraints of EU membership removed.

> **Box 5.1** **UKIP leader Nigel Farage on a 'No' vote to Europe**
>
> As someone who is going to be arguing very firmly that No, Britain's future does not lie inside the European Union, I am unashamedly optimistic about the potential that lies ahead of Britain as an independent nation. I have, after all, spent much of my adult life making the case as to why Britain would not just survive, but indeed thrive, once free from the shackles of Brussels. Perhaps the most common misconception people have about the anti-EU position is that our argument represents some form of isolationism. Nothing could be further from the truth in fact. This referendum campaign is going to be about saying no to an outdated European model in favour of turning Britain into a thriving, energetic, global hub.
>
> Source: *Daily Telegraph*, 16 June 2015

The political consequences of staying in

This option would be much less dramatic than a vote to leave. Even so, the landscape of British politics would change in a number of ways:

- Both UKIP and the eurosceptic wing of the Conservative Party will have been outflanked by the popular vote, especially if there is a decisive result. Anti-European politicians will lose their authority to campaign against UK membership.
- The UK will still have the problem of what to do about immigration while the UK's borders are still open to the rest of the EU.
- At least the government will feel more able to deal with its European counterparts, knowing that UK membership is more secure.
- On the other hand, the UK government's negotiating position in Europe may be weakened as the threat of withdrawal could no longer be used (Box 5.2).
- At some stage in the future, the issue of whether to adopt the euro as the UK's currency will have to be faced.

Box 5.2 David Cameron on British membership of the EU

David Cameron comments on his intentions to renegotiate British membership of the EU:

> Our membership of the EU will once again have a common market at its heart. We would have got off the treadmill to ever-closer union. We'd have addressed the issue of migration to Britain from the rest of the EU. We'd have protected Britain's place in the single market for the long term. It will not be the status quo. We will have fixed problems which have so frustrated the British people. It will be a new and different membership, one that is better for Britain and better for Europe, a membership rooted in what is our national interest today, a Britain in Europe, but not run by Europe.

> Source: speech to the European Council, 26 June 2015

Summary

Opinion polls are not as trustworthy as we once thought they were, given the margin of error they suffered from in the 2015 general election. Even so, it is interesting that, in the summer of 2015, in the *Daily Telegraph* 'poll tracker', an average of polls on how people intend to vote in the EU referendum, the numbers came out: **to stay in 53%, to leave 27%**, with the rest to make up their minds. This is quite a dramatic and clear indication of current opinion. As a word of warning, however, the polls also show that opinion on the issue is very volatile. For example, it may be that the recent flood of migrants from North Africa and the Middle East into southern Europe will strengthen opinion against membership, as this would allow the UK to strengthen its borders. There may be 2 years before the UK goes to the polls, so much can change before then. An opinion poll carried out by Survation in September 2015 showed 51% of respondents saying they would vote to leave the EU — the first such outcome for several years. The survey indicated that the migrant crisis was the cause of this shift in opinion.

Whatever happens, the referendum will be the most momentous decision to be made in the UK since the last referendum in 1975, though Scots will rightly argue that their own referendum on independence was more important for them. A 'Yes' vote will remove the issue from UK politics for a generation; a 'No' vote will fundamentally alter the UK's position in the world.

Exam focus

To consolidate your knowledge of this chapter, answer the following questions:

1 Why is a referendum to be held on UK membership of the EU by 2017?
2 Assess the impact of the rise of UKIP in UK politics.
3 Critically assess the arguments for the UK remaining in the EU.
4 Critically assess the arguments for the UK leaving the EU.
5 Assess the impact on UK politics of a decision to leave the EU.

Chapter 6

The Lib Dems: the end or can Tim Farron save them?

Context

The Liberal Democrat Party came into existence in 1988. It was an amalgamation of two parties:

- **The Liberal Party** that had existed since the late nineteenth century and had been the party of such legendary leaders as William Gladstone, Herbert Asquith and David Lloyd George.
- **The Social Democratic Party (SDP)**, a much younger party that had come into existence in 1981. The SDP was formed from a group of Labour members who believed that the party under the leadership of Michael Foot had become far too left wing. Its key figures were known as the 'Gang of Four' (after a notorious group of plotters against Mao Zedong in China). They were Shirley Williams, David Owen, Bill Rodgers and Roy Jenkins.

The two parties fought the 1983 and 1987 general elections as separate parties, though they made agreements not to stand against each other in most constituencies. The arrangement between them was known as the **Liberal–SDP Alliance**.

The Alliance did well in the two elections in terms of votes, but not in terms of seats. Its performance was as follows:

Year	Seats won	% of national vote
1983	12	25.4
1987	22	22.6

Having failed to make a breakthrough, the two parties joined into one in 1988. After that the party made steady progress:

Year	Seats won	% of national votes
1992	20	17.8
1997	46	16.7
2001	52	18.3
2005	62	22.0
2010	57	23.0

The party, then led by Nick Clegg, went into coalition with the Conservative Party between 2010 and 2015. Then disaster came. In the 2015 election the party suffered something of a meltdown, winning only 8 seats on 7.9% of the popular vote — in other words, a complete reversal of the trend since 1992. The party also lost all but one of its seats in Scotland and lost all 15 of its seats in its former stronghold, southwest England. Though its leader, Nick Clegg, survived, just retaining his own Sheffield constituency, most of its leadership group lost their seats in Parliament. These included Danny Alexander (first secretary to the Treasury), Vince Cable (business secretary), David Laws, Lynne Featherstone, Simon Hughes and Ed Davey. Nick Clegg resigned immediately after the 2015 election and the party elected Tim Farron, one of its few remaining MPs, as its new leader.

There is a precedent for what happened to the Liberal Democrats which comes from Germany. The equivalent of the Liberal Democrats there is the Free Democrat Party (FDP). For most of the period after the Second World War the FDP has been the third party, often forming coalitions with either the Conservatives or the Social Democrats. In the German general election of 2009 the FDP achieved a high point of 14.6% of the popular vote, gaining 61 seats (Germany operates a partly proportional electoral system, so the party gained a fair share of the parliamentary seats). It formed a coalition with the Conservative government led by Angela Merkel. However, Germany, in common with much of the Western world, suffered an economic depression following the 2008 financial crash.

In a situation not unlike that faced by the Liberal Democrats in 2015, the FDP was wiped out in the 2013 general election. It failed to gain 5% of the popular vote which meant, under the German constitution, that it was not allowed *any* seats at all. Afterwards, Angela Merkel remarked: 'In a coalition it is always the small party that gets bashed.' She might just as well have been talking about the Liberal Democrats in 2015.

Why did the Liberal Democrats lose so badly?

There is not just one reason why this 'perfect storm' engulfed the party. Several causes can be identified. Among them are these:

- The leadership of Nick Clegg was discredited. This largely stemmed from his complete commitment to opposing rises in university tuition fees followed by his U-turn in agreeing to an increase to £9,000. The electorate do not like politicians who blatantly break their promises.

- The party as a whole was seen as weak in its dealings with the Conservatives. All its attempts to persuade the public that it had had a major impact on health, welfare, taxation and economic policy seemed to fail.
- Many voters clearly punished the Lib Dems for keeping the Conservative Party in power when it was unpopular in certain regions. This certainly occurred in Scotland, in London and in parts of the north of England.
- The Conservatives successfully targeted Liberal Democrat seats in the southwest of England, gaining all 15 of them. Here the message got through that it was the Conservatives who had rescued the economy, not the Liberal Democrats.
- Young voters abandoned the party on the grounds that it had sacrificed some of its radical principles (e.g. over human rights, constitutional reform and the environment) for the sake of remaining in power. Many of these votes went to the Greens in England and the SNP in Scotland.

Perhaps, though, Angela Merkel had it right. A small party in coalition is in a 'no-win' situation. It will always be criticised for making compromises with the larger party, but it will not gain the credit for what the government has done well.

Who is Tim Farron?

Farron was 45 years old when he was elected leader of the Liberal Democrats. He is a family man, married with four children. He was elected the MP for Westmorland and Lonsdale in 2005 and held the seat in 2015 with a majority of nearly 9,000, very much against the trend on the night. He is a committed Christian, but does not wish to be defined by his religious convictions, though he accepts that his Christianity informs his political beliefs.

He studied politics at university, was a member of the housing pressure group Shelter and went on to work as a university administrator before standing for Parliament. As a younger man, he was a member of a rock band and harboured hopes of a career in the music business. Between 1993 and 1999 he was a local councillor in Lancashire.

Between 2010 and 2015 he was president of the Liberal Democrat Party, a largely honorary position. He has often been seen as something of an outsider in the party, a leader of the 'left wing' (though he describes himself as 'centrist'). He was never part of Nick Clegg's inner leadership group. In the coalition government he did not have a ministerial post — a fact that may work in his favour in the long run.

Where does Tim Farron stand politically?

Farron set out his political beliefs in his acceptance speech following his election as party leader on 16 July 2015.

In an echo of the 1942 Beveridge Report, a document inspired by a leading Liberal of the day, he said this:

> And lives needed changing, a difference needed to be made. I learnt at first hand
> that nothing robs you of your freedom like poverty and poor housing. I also

learnt that dependency can stifle freedom just as much. I saw the potential for people to change their own lives if only we gave them the freedom to learn, the freedom to earn, the freedom to be the best they can be.

This passage suggests that he wants to see the party defend the benefits system, reward enterprise and build many more houses. To those who say that such state intervention is against liberal principles of promoting freedom, he is suggesting, as Beveridge did, that the cause of freedom is best served by giving people more control over their lives and by removing deprivation.

Farron also demonstrated staunch support for a liberal attitude towards immigration, a direct challenge to UKIP and the right wing of the Conservative Party:

And we do that [support controlled immigration] because we value the contribution every single individual has to make to this beautiful country of ours. As the world changes around us, we see the opportunities and not just the dangers, because we see the best in people. We trust people.

Farron is considered to be in the centre ground of his party's policies but his general statement on rights and on challenging vested interests and concentrations of power looks fairly radical:

That's why we stand up for the individual against the state. Why we stand up for the minority against the majority. Why we stand up for the outsider against the establishment. Because that is not just what we do, it is who we are.

He is also clear that he wants to see strong local government restored and to see his party renew its commitment to protecting the environment:

And community politics is about mobilising our communities to build the homes that we need, to win a local battle in the war against climate change, to get the resources to strengthen our schools. I want more MPs, and before that, I want hundreds and hundreds of new Liberal Democrat councillors, immersed in their communities, living their values by getting things done. Step by step, we will change people's lives for the better and as we do that we will regain their trust. You see, our survival, revival, our rebirth, our rebuild, will happen in communities, in councils, in common rooms, away from the stuffy corridors of Westminster and Whitehall.

Now free from the constraints of being in coalition, Farron launched a direct and vitriolic attack on conservatism:

If you care about human rights, join us. If you think you shouldn't have your e-mails snooped on, join us. If you think everyone deserves a decent home, join us. If you think it is wrong to demonise immigrants, the young, the poor, foreigners, Brussels, the English, the Scots, join us. If you are fed up of self-satisfied politicians, ambitious for themselves and unambitious for their country, then guess what…you are a liberal. Embrace that diagnosis. It is an utterly decent and British condition so join us, join today.

In practice, Farron has identified his priorities as party leader. These include:

- A strong defence of civil liberties in the UK (he sees himself very much as a traditional liberal in this regard). He will vigorously oppose the replacement of the European Convention on Human Rights with a British Bill of Rights. He will also oppose measures against terrorism which threaten civil liberties.
- On economic policy he tends to favour the use of higher income taxes on the wealthy (while reducing tax for low income groups) in order to create more equality and to reduce the government deficit.
- He will campaign for the UK to remain in the European Union in the forthcoming referendum.
- He favours a positive, liberal approach to immigration, seeing it as an important element in making Britain a diverse and dynamic society. He also recognises the positive contribution that immigrants play in economic growth. In the current migration crisis he argues for Britain taking in a fair share of the migrants.
- He believes the National Health Service should direct more of its resources to the treatment of mental health problems after what he sees as many years of neglect.
- Representing, as he does, a largely rural community, he wants to prioritise the needs of such areas in government policy.
- He is a strong environmentalist. He champions what Liberal Democrats call the 'Green Economy', which means that economic policies must always have the protection of the environment as their basis. He favours more investment in renewable energy generation. This is part of his policy to force Britain to conform to strict targets on reducing harmful emissions. He is opposed to fracking.
- He is a supporter of LGBT rights, though there were indications that he was less than enthusiastic about same-sex marriage.
- He is opposed to the renewal of the Trident nuclear missile system.
- He stresses the need for Britain to build more affordable housing.
- He is opposed to the 'bedroom tax' — a restriction on housing benefits for those with unused bedrooms in their homes. He voted against it, against the party's policy.
- Above all, perhaps, **Farron voted against the rise in university tuition fees in December 2010**. He said at the time that integrity was more important than power. This may well stand him in good stead as Nick Clegg's successor. He remains opposed to tuition fees.

Can the Liberal Democrats recover?

Superficially it would appear that they cannot, that their 2015 defeat was so severe that it will be a mortal blow to the party. They have lost the whole of their leadership group and most of their MPs. However, there are factors which may now actually work in their favour. Table 6.1 presents an assessment of Liberal Democrat prospects.

Table 6.1 An assessment of Liberal Democrat prospects

Negative indications	Positive indications
The credibility of the party may have been irreparably damaged for a generation by the experience of coalition government and election defeat	As the saying goes, when you are at the bottom, the only way is up
With only eight MPs the party will make little impact on parliamentary politics	The Liberal Democrats still have strong representation in local government
The UK may well be heading for a period of Conservative domination (see Chapter 2)	The disarray in the Labour Party presents the Liberal Democrats with an opportunity to become the more effective opposition party
Tim Farron is an inexperienced leader	Farron is not tainted with the experience of coalition as he was not a minister. He also voted against the rise in university tuition fees — a policy and broken promise that proved tremendously unpopular with the electorate
If Labour does recover its position, the Liberal Democrats may be squeezed out	The Liberal Democrats do not appear to have lost members as a result of defeat (indeed there has been an increase in membership) and still have a strong organisation on the ground

Summary

The future fortunes of the Liberal Democrat Party probably depend largely on the fortunes of Labour. The centre-left of UK politics is now fragmented with the SNP, the Labour Party, the Green Party, Plaid Cymru and the Liberal Democrats all representing anti-Conservative forces in the country.

The Liberal Democrats could certainly benefit from a collapse in Labour support as well as some defections from Labour following the election of Jeremy Corbyn as party leader. It may even be that the Labour Party will split on a left–right basis, in which case there will be room for cooperation between the Liberal Democrats and some sections of Labour. There is no great difference between the policies of the Liberal Democrats and those of mainstream Labour. The party will also benefit from the fact that Tim Farron is not carrying the burden of having served in the coalition government.

However, a different scenario could also present itself. This is that the party goes into long-term decline and returns to where the Liberal Party stood in the period 1945–79 when it had a small number of seats, was a small radical group of MPs and made no significant impact on UK politics.

Exam focus

To consolidate your knowledge of this chapter, answer the following questions:

1 What are the main policies of the Liberal Democrat Party in 2015?
2 To what extent, and in what ways, can the Liberal Democrats today be considered a 'left-wing' party?
3 What are the main issues of conflict between Liberal Democrat policies and those of the current government?
4 Why did the Liberal Democrats fare so badly in the 2015 general election?
5 What is the role of the 'third party' in UK politics?

Chapter 7

George Osborne's Northern Powerhouse: a new era in local government?

Exam success

The up-to-date facts, examples and arguments in this chapter will help you to produce good quality answers in your AS unit tests in the following areas of the specification:

Edexcel	AQA	OCR
Unit 1	**Unit 1**	**Unit F851**
Party policies and ideas	Political parties	Political parties
Unit 2	**Unit 2**	**Unit F852**
The constitution	Multi-level governance	The constitution

Context

The Conservative Party has always been thought of as primarily a centralising party — it has traditionally believed in the idea that central, rather than local, government should be the driving force of economic development in the UK. This belief also had a political dimension in that Conservatives have often faced opposition from Labour and Liberal Democrat strongholds in local government. Labour in particular has usually controlled government in such cities as Birmingham, Leeds, Sheffield, Newcastle, Liverpool and Manchester, with occasional intervals of Liberal Democrat control. Furthermore, these Labour strongholds have often been dominated by left-wing elements, including trade unionists. Small wonder, then, that the Conservatives have been wary of giving local government too much autonomous power.

Set against this, there has been growing concern that the UK economy has become unbalanced — that it is too centred on London and the south and is over-reliant on service industries based predominantly in the south, and not enough in the midlands and the north of England. This problem has been recognised by the chancellor of the exchequer, George Osborne. In recent years, therefore, he has introduced the idea of a 'Northern Hub' — a new area of economic development based on Manchester, but also involving Leeds, Sheffield, Liverpool and Birmingham.

The economic dimension

The upgrading of infrastructure has also been dubbed the **Northern Hub**. A number of major infrastructure projects have been announced, many of which are already under way. Among them are the following:

- High Speed 2 (HS2) is a huge plan to upgrade the railway system, at first from London to Birmingham and then on to the northern cities. This is highly controversial, not least because of its cost which is estimated at anything between £40 billion and £80 billion. It will take probably until 2033 to complete, with the first phase to Birmingham ready in 2026. This will considerably reduce journey times between these destinations.
- Northern electrification has already begun, with £600 million being spent to improve rail connections across the whole of the north of England.
- An upgrade of Manchester airport is now proposed, costing £1 billion and due for completion in 2023.

It is hoped that these proposals will reduce unemployment and reliance on welfare benefits in areas where there has traditionally been economic stagnation, especially since the decline of manufacturing industries in the 1970s and 1980s.

The political dimension

Some commentators have described Osborne's plans for a Northern Powerhouse as a form of regional devolution. Apart from his announcements on economic development he also wishes to devolve more powers to city regions. The focus of his attention lies in Greater Manchester, though Leeds, Sheffield, Birmingham, Newcastle and Liverpool are likely to follow.

There is no doubt that Osborne and the government hope that this will have a political as well as an economic dividend. It may well end the Conservative problem of being seen as a predominantly 'southern' party. By spreading a sense of economic wellbeing more widely, Osborne hopes that his party will be able to spread its appeal.

The main ways in which devolution to the cities will work are contained in the Cities and Local Government Devolution Bill, which was introduced into Parliament in 2015.

The Cities and Local Government Devolution Bill

This bill which is sponsored by George Osborne is making its way through the House of Commons, having already passed through the Lords, and will become law in 2016. Its main provisions are as follows:

- To receive more devolved powers cities must introduce an elected mayor. Without an elected mayor devolution will be denied.
- Elected city mayors will have similar powers to those exercised by the London mayor. These will include control of local transport, housing, planning and policing. The mayor will also have powers to oversee economic development

in his or her region. To facilitate this, the new devolved authorities may also be granted limited borrowing powers.

■ The system of government in each devolved city will have to be adjusted so as to place the elected mayor at the centre. Any proposed system will require the approval of the secretary of state for communities and local government.

■ The new local government units will be single tier, i.e. the city government will govern the whole city and the region that surrounds it. There will be no subordinate units of local government.

■ There will also be a possibility, with ministerial approval, of the new devolved city regions taking over some of the functions of the NHS.

■ Greater Manchester will be the first such authority to come into existence in 2017. The system of government it adopts will be used as a 'blueprint' for other new city regions to follow.

■ At the Conservative Party conference in October 2015, Osborne also announced that he would devolve power to local authorities over business rates. These are local taxes levied on commercial premises. They have long been controversial as they are often too high for businesses to thrive and because they have been centrally controlled. He will allow local government to vary these rates and will also give them control over the revenue. The plan represents the devolution of £26 billion per annum to local councils away from central government.

The bill, soon to be an Act, contains relatively little certainty as so many of the potentially devolved powers will require the approval of central government. In other words, the new elected mayors may *appear* to have considerable powers, but in practice may not be in a position to achieve very much. Indeed some critics have suggested that this is largely a 'cosmetic exercise' in devolution.

Box 7.1 George Osborne on elected city mayors

It's right people have a single point of accountability. Someone they elect, who takes the decisions and carries the can. So with these new powers for cities must come new city-wide elected mayors who work with local councils. I will not impose this model on anyone. But nor will I settle for less. London has a mayor, Greater Manchester has agreed to have a mayor as part of our northern powerhouse — and this new law will make that happen.

The issue of elected mayors

The most interesting feature of the changes is the introduction of city mayors (Box 7.1). As things stand, the office of 'mayor' is largely ceremonial. The new elected mayors would certainly have more powers, but there are question marks over whether the new system will be more democratic. Table 7.1 details the advantages and disadvantages of elected mayors in city regions. Several conclusions are based on London's experience of having an elected mayor.

Table 7.1 An assessment of elected city mayors

Advantages of elected mayors	Disadvantages of elected mayors
They can be a figurehead for a city and create a sense of unity and purpose. The mayors will also be able to 'promote' their cities to the outside world	There is a danger that election turnouts will be low, so the legitimacy of the mayor's position will be questionable
As their election will create more interest and attention, the mayors may be more accountable than local councils currently are	The powers devolved to the mayors will not be entrenched, so they could be overruled by central government
The elected mayors will be continuously accountable to the elected authority and this will be more transparent than is currently the case	If a mayor is from a different party to that which controls central government, there will be conflict between the centre and city regions
Though it remains uncertain, elected mayors will be able to use their enhanced powers in a way that is more sensitive to local needs, especially in such fields as policing, planning, health and housing	Some may argue that the proposal will put too much power into the hands of one person instead of a larger council and its committees
It is assumed that the new system will create a boost for local investment and therefore economic development in the region	

Other political views

The Liberal Democrats have long supported the transfer of more powers to local government and so they are in favour of city devolution. They, like Labour (before Jeremy Corbyn), support the idea but would wish to go further, especially in the fields of health and education. Jeremy Corbyn, however, has called the proposals a 'cruel deception'. He suggests that the government is using the proposals to disguise the fact that it is cutting investment in such areas as policing, housing, health and education. By devolving responsibility to cities, he argues, it will deflect attention away from the fact that *national* funding is being squeezed.

As a traditional socialist thinker, Corbyn naturally tends towards centralisation of state provision. This perspective sees centralisation of provision as essential to creating equality. If too much power is granted to local government, there is a danger that different regions will suffer from excessive variation in the quality of services and in economic development. He suggests that a national plan for regeneration is needed. On the other hand, Corbyn is also not opposed to devolution 'in principle'. To work effectively though, he argues, regions must be granted realistic levels of economic support from the centre.

Meanwhile Nigel Farage of UKIP calls city devolution 'putting the cart before the horse'. By this he means the UK must sort out the relationship between England, Wales, Scotland and Northern Ireland before worrying about the English regions.

The SNP and Plaid Cymru, not surprisingly, scoff at city devolution. They consider Wales and Scotland to have suffered discrimination when state resources are being distributed. Having claimed that England has considerable advantages, they are hardly likely to be interested in power being transferred to English cities. In fact, it may well be that Osborne's proposals will further stoke up demands for home rule in those two countries.

Summary

As things stand at the end of 2015, the prospects for a 'new era of local government' remain unclear. Certainly the idea of single city regional government is a new one, but it will only be meaningful if these regions have significant powers devolved to them. Manchester will be the key. If things go well there and the new system achieves widespread public approval, it may well be copied elsewhere.

In Chapter 4 of this update we asked the question whether a federal UK is inevitable. The answer was that it remained very unlikely. There is no reason to believe that this change will make any difference to that view. Transferring some powers from Whitehall to elected mayors does not have any great constitutional significance. It also has to be said that it is really only reverting to a degree of local government power that already existed before the 1980s when Margaret Thatcher exerted an increased level of centralised control.

Whether it succeeds in rebalancing the UK economy remains to be seen. In the past it has proved very difficult to promote economic growth in those regions that were formerly the 'engine' of manufacturing in the UK, but which have now lost much of their economic base. Trying to 're-attach' the north to the south of England is an audacious policy by Osborne and one which requires massive public and private investment.

Exam focus

To consolidate your knowledge of this chapter, answer the following questions:

1 To what extent is city devolution 'real' devolution?
2 Why does the Conservative government wish to strengthen local government in cities?
3 Can elected mayors improve local democracy?
4 Distinguish between city devolution and federalism.

Chapter 8

The welfare state: is it in danger?

Exam success

The up-to-date facts, examples and arguments in this chapter will help you to produce good quality answers in your AS unit tests in the following areas of the specification:

Edexcel	AQA	OCR
Unit 1	**Unit 1**	**Unit F851**
Party policies and ideas	Political parties	Political parties

Context

Before we can consider its current position in Britain it is necessary first to establish what actually constitutes the term '**welfare state**'. Its principles are as follows:

- All taxpaying citizens must contribute to it through general taxation and National Insurance. In other words, nobody is allowed to opt out of paying.
- All citizens are entitled to the benefits offered under the welfare state.
- On the whole, the benefits of the welfare state should be free at the point of delivery. This principle has been eroded to some extent, notably in the case of dental treatment and medical prescriptions, but it is mostly intact.

Some have argued that it is a basic principle that the state should be responsible for *supplying* the various services, while others disagree. It is certainly true that many services have been 'contracted out' to the private sector, but this does not mean that the private enterprises involved are permitted to charge for what they produce.

There are four senses in which we should consider whether the welfare state is in danger. These are:

- Is the scope of the welfare state being eroded? In other words, is it less extensive than it used to be?
- Are people being asked to contribute too much to services to maintain the claim that it is free?
- Is the benefits system being cut so much that it will become largely ineffective in acting as a safety net for those in most need?
- Does the widespread use of the public sector actually constitute 'privatisation'?

The scope of the welfare state

On the whole, the picture here is positive for the welfare state. The key areas of healthcare, education and social security remain largely intact. Indeed the provision in these areas has, if anything, expanded since the 1940s.

On the other hand, there are some welfare areas that now appear to be in decline. Among them are social security, social care and social housing.

Health

Many more treatments are now available through the NHS, including such areas as end-of-life care (hospices), in vitro fertilisation (IVF), some cosmetic surgery and a range of so-called 'alternative' medicines such as acupuncture and reflexology.

Table 8.1 shows health spending as a proportion of GDP since 1980. We can see that there has been a dramatic increase since 2000, reflecting increasing concern that this is a key area of government responsibility. This also reflects the willingness of governments to recognise the effects of an ageing population together with the greater availability of expensive treatments by increasing spending relative to economic growth.

Table 8.1 Health spending as a proportion of UK GDP, 1980–2014

Year	% of GDP
1980	4.2
1990	4.6
1995	5.3
2000	5.3
2005	7.0
2010	8.4
2014	9.1

Source: OECD

Education

Entitlement to education has spread to 3 and 4 year olds and the state now provides families with support for nursery care. There are also now plans to provide free school meals for all, not just deprived, pupils in certain age groups.

Although there is now a new range of school types, including free schools and academies, many of which are outside local authority control, all of them are free and no state school is allowed to charge for its services (some ask for voluntary contributions). The same is true of tertiary colleges, but not universities and other higher education institutions. Table 8.2 shows that there has been no erosion in education spending and that in fact it has gradually increased. Expenditure *per head* has also not changed significantly.

Table 8.2 Education as a proportion of UK GDP, 1980–2014

Year	% of GDP
1980	5.5
1990	4.8
1995	5.0
2000	4.6
2005	5.5
2010	6.3
2014	6.3

Source: OECD

Social security

Most of the social security system is intact. However, it has been eroded in some areas. There is an overall cap on how much a family can claim, child benefits have been reduced for large families, unemployment benefit has been replaced by jobseeker's allowance and disability benefit has become more difficult to claim. However, the key benefits remain, notably the state pension, which will soon be rising significantly, tax credits, family benefits, sick pay and support for those who cannot find employment.

Table 8.3 shows how social security benefit payments have increased as a proportion of GDP. These figures are affected by key factors such as unemployment levels (falling in recent years) and the demands on old age pensions (the UK population is ageing significantly), but they do indicate that there has been no severe reduction in the provision of benefits.

Table 8.3 Social security benefits as a proportion of UK GDP, 1980–2014

Year	% of GDP
1980	16.3
1990	16.3
2000	18.4
2005	20.2
2010	22.8
2014	21.7

Source: OECD

Social care

Care in old age has been reduced and individuals are now expected to contribute to their own care if they have a reasonable income and/or assets such as their own home. Such people have to fall back on totally private provision or contribute to local authority care homes from their own income.

Social housing

Assessments of this aspect should be treated with some caution. Since the 1980s local authority house building and renting has declined sharply. However, some of the fall has been taken up by housing associations. These are non-profit-making voluntary associations which exist to provide low-rent housing. Housing associations are also subsidised by central government. Therefore it could be argued that they are part of the 'welfare state'. Whether they are or not remains an open question. This update assumes they are not.

The construction of local authority homes has declined dramatically, from a peak of 159,000 per annum in 1967, to 77,000 in 1980. Since then the fall has been even steeper, down to just over 3,000 in 2014. This appears to show a collapse in this sector.

Social housing is housing provided by local authorities and housing associations. Table 8.4 shows the fall in the proportion of home occupation accounted for by social housing since 1981. The provision of subsidised housing for rent by the state has declined seriously. Increasingly people are expected to buy their own home, or rent from housing associations. This has been for two reasons. First, considerably less housing is being built by local authorities and housing associations. Second, the 'right to buy' scheme, which has run since the early 1980s, has meant that much council housing has been sold to its tenants but not replaced by new housing. In 2015 the new Conservative government announced a policy of allowing housing association tenants to buy their own home at a subsidised price. If this policy is implemented (it does have considerable opposition), experts in the field suggest that it will reduce social housing stock even further.

Table 8.4 Proportion of people renting from local authorities or housing associations, 1981–2013

Year	% of total population in social housing
1981	31
2011	18
2013	16

Source: ONS

Contributions to the welfare state

On the whole, the welfare state is still financed from general taxation, including National Insurance. Charging for NHS prescriptions dates back to the 1950s, so it is not a new phenomenon and has not increased excessively since it was first introduced. Proposals to charge patients for visits to the GP have been advanced in recent years but have always been resisted and there are now no plans to introduce such payments.

The main erosions of the principle have occurred in care in old age, dental care and higher education:

- Those who need care in old age must contribute or pay the full cost, depending on their income and/or assets.
- Patients now have to make a large contribution to dental care and must pay the full cost of cosmetic work.
- Tuition fees of up to £9,000 per annum have been introduced and are expected to rise further. In the past, university and degree level education has been free and grants or loans have been available for living expenses. Tuition fees have proved to be the most corrosive of policies in relation to the welfare state.

Prescription charges, dental charges and tuition fees are, however, exceptions. In principle, all taxpayers have to contribute and the principle that services are free remains. Furthermore, where there are charges, those who can show they are on low incomes, or are young or old, and in a few other circumstances such as pregnancy, do receive the services absolutely free. For example, it is estimated that about half of all NHS patients can claim free prescriptions.

Cutting the benefits system

There are several examples of benefits cuts which have been made in recent years, particularly since 2010. There are also more cuts in the pipeline from the 2015 budget. The main examples have been as follows:
- A cap on total benefits received by a family is being reduced to £23,000 per annum in London and £20,000 elsewhere.
- The 'bedroom tax' means that any family in receipt of housing benefit will lose benefit proportionally for any bedrooms they have which are vacant.
- Child benefit has been removed where a parent is earning over £50,000 per annum.
- The income limit above which tax credits can be claimed has been nearly halved and tax credits cannot be claimed for more than two children.
- 18–21 years olds are no longer entitled to housing benefit.

This represents an erosion of the *universal* nature of the benefits system and will affect the poor disproportionally, but there has not been any actual *removal* of benefits. In other words, it is a matter of *scale* rather than *scope*.

So-called privatisation

A strict definition of privatisation would be that services were being supplied by the private sector and were being paid for at the point of delivery rather than being financed out of general taxation. There is, of course, widespread private welfare provision, including education, housing, pensions, social and healthcare, but nobody is allowed to opt out of taxation and National Insurance because they are using private provision rather than that supplied by the state. In this sense there has been no privatisation of the welfare state. However, when politicians and other groups refer to the term 'privatisation', what they actually mean is the *involvement* of the private sector in supplying welfare services. There are certainly increasing examples of this, which include:

- The NHS increasingly 'buys in' services from private healthcare providers, mainly private hospitals and clinics.
- Private investors are often invited to build schools, hospitals and the like in schemes called private finance initiatives (PFIs). Here the state does not have to make the initial investment but pays interest and other fees to private providers.
- Most old age care homes are now privately run, receiving a combination of income from their clients and from local authorities.
- Some social care is being provided by private agencies paid for from public funds.

Opponents of these developments point to a number of issues:
- They are eroding the 'public service ethos' of the welfare state, making people clients rather than citizens.
- Private sector organisations seek to make profits which may divert resources away from frontline care.
- The private sector is more difficult to regulate. This is especially important as the need for the private sector to engage in competition may result in lower quality.
- They are a 'Trojan Horse' to full-scale privatisation. In other words, once the state becomes used to using the private sector it will be a small step to allowing it to replace the welfare state altogether.

Summary

Warnings about the impending demise of the welfare state have been with us for some time. However, the statistics suggest that there has been no major erosion in welfare provision in the UK, with the possible exception of social housing and higher education. Furthermore, none of the mainstream parties has adopted policies that threaten the *principle* of the welfare state, with the possible exception of UKIP, which is much more supportive of private sector provision of welfare than other parties.

The Conservative Party is committed to reducing welfare expenditure, especially the benefits system, but this is partly to do with deficit reduction. There is no suggestion that state healthcare, education or social insurance will be fundamentally threatened. It is also true that there has been increased use of the private sector in welfare, notably in healthcare, but this does not amount to 'privatisation' because the service is still financed from general taxation and is largely free at the point of delivery.

What may be under threat is the notion that the welfare state, particularly the benefits system, should be used to redistribute real income and reduce relative deprivation. Conservatives see the benefits system as a safety net, reserved only for those who are not capable of supporting themselves (such as the seriously disabled and long-term chronically ill and those who have to rely on low-paid employment), rather than as a means of reducing inequality — a policy supported by Labour, the SNP, Plaid Cymru, the Greens and the Liberal Democrats.

Exam focus

To consolidate your knowledge of this chapter, answer the following questions:

1 To what extent has the welfare state been privatised?
2 To what extent is the Conservative Party still committed to the welfare state?
3 What are the main conflicts between UK parties concerning the welfare state?
4 To what extent is there a consensus in the UK concerning the welfare state?

Chapter 9

Green politics: now established in the UK?

Context

The main vehicle for the promotion of environmental issues in the UK is the Green Party. This was founded in 1985, though it was, in effect, largely a name change from the Ecology Party that had already existed for 10 years. Since 1985 the Green Party has made slow but positive progress in terms of votes won at general elections. Its general election performance is shown in the table below.

Year	Performance
1987	0.3%
1992	0.5%
1997	0.3%
2001	0.6%
2005	1.0%
2010	0.9%
2015	3.8%

However, we need to go back to 1989 to identify the principal breakthrough for the green movement. In that year there were elections to the European Parliament and the Green Party won 2.3 million votes, representing 14.9% of the total and coming third behind the Conservatives and Labour. The event had a dramatic effect. The other main parties all realised that environmental issues had now come to the forefront of popular sentiment. As a result, all three national parties adopted policies that were designed to recognise this change.

Another breakthrough year was 2015. The Green Party had won its first parliamentary seat in Brighton in 2010, when its then leader, Caroline Lucas, was elected, but a share of the vote of 3.8% in 2015 was a significant success even though the party was not able to add to its one seat.

At the same time as the Green Party was making slow but steady progress, the number and size of environmental pressure groups was increasing. Interest in environmental issues should not just be measured in terms of election votes, but also in people's participation in such issues. Some of the most important pressure groups in the field include:

- Greenpeace
- Friends of the Earth
- The National Trust
- World Wide Fund for Nature
- Royal Society for the Protection of Birds (RSPB)
- Women's Environmental Network
- Campaign to Protect Rural England

In addition to these national, long-term campaign groups there are now many organisations dedicated to pursuing specific aims in the environmental field. Prominent examples include **Frack Off** (anti-fracking), **Plane Stupid** (against airport expansion) and **STOP HS2** (against the creation of a new high speed rail line from London to Birmingham and the north). At any particular moment, there are also hundreds of local groups working to protect their community's environment on a smaller scale.

Furthermore, campaign groups have had some notable successes in recent years. For example, the expansion of Heathrow airport has been delayed and is now in jeopardy as a result of the federation of groups dedicated to stopping development on the site. Fracking, too, has been delayed and plans for new sites have been held up in planning disputes. The organised cycling lobby has begun to have successes in persuading city councils, not least in London, to provide them with safe lanes and better protection from vehicular traffic, while the National Trust and the RSPB have been able to block plans to erode the countryside and British forests for housing and industrial development.

One further development is worthy of mention. This is the fact that the Green Party has now developed a full set of policies across the whole range of government responsibilities. This programme is radical both politically and environmentally.

Green Party policies in 2015

The Green Party introduced a full-scale manifesto in 2015. Its main proposals are outlined here.

The economy

- Increase public spending to almost half of national income
- Close taxation loopholes and crack down on tax avoidance
- Introduce a wealth tax of 1–2% on people worth £3 million or more
- Salaries above £150,000 a year to incur a 60% income tax rate
- Introduce a financial transaction tax (a 'Robin Hood' tax) on banks

- Increase the national minimum wage to a living wage for all, of £10 per hour by 2020
- Create 1 million new well-paid public sector jobs
- Reduce National Insurance contributions
- Ensure the highest wage in any business is no more than ten times the lowest

The environment and transport
- Ban fracking for shale gas
- Phase out coal-fired power and stop new nuclear reactors
- A public programme of renewables, flood defences and home insulation
- £35 billion in public investment in renewable power over the next parliament
- Tackle emissions by scrapping the government's national roads building programme
- Subsidise public transport and return the railways to national ownership
- Stop airport expansion
- Invest in electric vehicle charging

Housing
- Abolish the 'bedroom tax'
- Provide 500,000 social rented homes by 2020
- Bring empty homes back into use
- Cap rents, introduce longer tenancies and license landlords to provide greater protection to renters

Health
- End the 'creeping privatisation' of the NHS and repeal the government's Health and Social Care Act 2012
- Increase the overall NHS budget by £12 billion a year to overcome the current 'funding crisis'
- Increase resources for mental health to make it a greater priority

Education
- Scrap university tuition fees and invest £1.5 billion extra a year in further education
- Bring academies and free schools into the local authority system
- Introduce a free but voluntary universal early education and childcare service from birth to 7 years old
- Restore the education maintenance allowance for 16 and 17 year olds

Other policies
The party also proposed the cancellation of such high expenditure projects as the renewal of Trident and the HS2 plan, using the resulting savings to finance some of its tax cuts and expenditure commitments.

Given the wide range of radical policies proposed by the Green Party, it is difficult to establish the extent to which the increase in voting for the party reflects a growing concern with environmental issues as opposed to support for its more general ideas. For example, the policy to scrap university tuition fees is bound to be popular with the young, whatever their views on the environment may be.

How green are the other parties?

All political parties in modern Britain must at least pay lip service to environmental issues and all have coherent policies in the area. This is largely a case of green issues not being a vote winner, but a lack of concern for the environment being a vote loser. Table 9.1 shows where the parties stood at the time of the 2015 general election on various environmental issues.

Table 9.1 Party positions on key environmental issues, May 2015

Issue	Conservative	Labour*	Lib. Dem.	UKIP
Renewable energy	The party will no longer subsidise onshore wind farms	Wind farms to be encouraged but mostly offshore	Enthusiastic about wind farms and other forms of renewable energy	Generally opposed to more wind farms
Emissions targets	Remains committed to international agreements	Carbon-free energy production by 2030	Totally zero-carbon Britain by 2050. Low targets for vehicles by 2040	Does not support emissions targets
Fracking	Strongly wishes to promote this technology	Supports its development but with strong regulations	Supports 'sensitive' development	Very much in favour
Nuclear energy	Has plans to build new plants and renew existing ones	In favour of increasing nuclear energy production as part of a low-carbon energy plan	Same as Labour	Same as the other parties
Others	Hopes to double cycling and will invest to make this possible All cars to have zero emissions by 2050	Very large investment in low-carbon energy technology A green investment bank to be set up to support small and medium businesses in the field of carbon reduction	Introduce low emission zones in towns and cities National Nature Parks to protect green spaces	The green belts to be protected

*Labour policy is extremely fluid. These were main policies at the time of the 2015 election

Table 9.1 demonstrates two features. One is that all parties, with the possible exception of UKIP, take environmental policies seriously and have comprehensive

plans to reduce emissions, promote low-carbon technologies, support fracking with strong regulations and promote the further development of nuclear energy.

The second feature is that there is a high degree of **consensus** on these issues. It is true that the Green Party on the left and UKIP on the right break this consensus in certain areas, but on the whole it is extensive. The main policy area where there is significant conflict concerns investment in wind farms and renewables in general. The Conservatives now wish to withdraw state support for research and investment, believing that these industries must freely compete in the market place without state subsidy, while the other parties wish to continue state investment and subsidy.

Summary

There is no doubt that 'green politics' is now firmly established in the UK. However, there are also several senses in which it remains only marginal as a political issue:

- Despite growing support and its first seat at Westminster in 2010, the Green Party has failed to make an electoral breakthrough at national level.
- Voters consistently tell polling researchers that the environment remains low on their list of priorities and is unlikely to affect the way they vote.
- As we have seen in recent years, when governments feel the need to reduce public spending, as has been the case since 2008, expenditure on the environment has proved to be a 'soft' target.

Nevertheless it is also true that political parties ignore such issues at their peril. Young voters in particular still wish to see environmentally-friendly policies to the forefront. If the main parties allow such policies to slip out of their plans, the Green Party will start to make inroads into their support.

Exam focus

To consolidate your knowledge of this chapter, answer the following questions:

1 To what extent is there consensus in the UK over environmental policy?
2 What are the main issues of conflict between parties in the UK concerning the environment?
3 To what extent is the environment a key political issue in UK politics?
4 Is the Green Party now a 'main' party in the UK?

Civil liberties: are they under threat in the UK?

Exam success

The up-to-date facts, examples and arguments in this chapter will help you to produce good quality answers in your AS unit tests in the following areas of the specification:

Edexcel	AQA	OCR
Unit 2	**Unit 2**	**Unit F852**
Judges and civil liberties	The British constitution	The judiciary

Context

The last few years of the twentieth century saw a Labour government enact a series of measures all designed to protect civil liberties in the UK. These included:

- **Data Protection Act 1998.** This Act recognised that an increasing amount of information about individuals was being held in digital form. This was seen as a danger to people's privacy and opened them to the possibility of false information being available too widely. To counter this, the legislation allowed people to view information being held about them and to have any errors corrected. It also restricted the ability of bodies holding such information to publicise it without authorisation.
- **Human Rights Act 1998.** This was the most dramatic piece of legislation protecting rights and liberties in the UK in modern history. It brought the **European Convention on Human Rights (ECHR)** into UK law. The ECHR guaranteed a whole range of rights and liberties such as privacy, right to a private life, right to life, and freedom of movement, expression and association. The terms of the ECHR must be enforced by the courts in the UK and the actions of government or any public body must not infringe the convention. Only the UK Parliament can pass legislation which might offend the ECHR, though it is not expected to do so.
- **Freedom of Information Act 2000.** This gave power to individuals and organisations to access information being held by any public body, largely local, regional and central government. The only exceptions are pieces of information that, if made public, might threaten national security.

The whole scene began to change, however, after 9/11, the terrorist attack on the World Trade Center in New York when nearly 3,000 were killed. A series of further attacks by terrorists intensified the calls for more measures to combat

such terrorism, even if these measures threatened civil liberties. The attacks on London in July 2007 added to the pressure.

While the debate about how far civil liberties can be sacrificed in the interests of national security continued, there was a rapid growth in telecommunications, both on the internet and through mobile phones. This growth in digital communications created both a problem and an opportunity for security services. The problem was that terrorist groups (as well as other criminal organisations) could now use the new systems to facilitate their activities. However, it also gave the authorities greater ability to monitor people's movements and communications.

The result has been a steady stream of legislation and other measures to combat crime and terrorism. The main examples are reviewed below.

Legislation that might have threatened civil liberties

Table 10.1 describes some of the main examples of such legislation and initiatives.

Table 10.1 Examples of legislation affecting civil liberties

Measure	Key provisions	Nature of the civil liberties threat
Regulation of Investigatory Powers Act 2000	Required internet service providers (ISPs) to provide information about encrypted messages passed between suspected terrorists. It also allowed the collection of metadata, i.e. the quantity of digital messages passing between people, though not its content	Intrusions into privacy
Terrorism Act 2006	Apart from creating new terrorism offences the Act created a new offence of disseminating material that might encourage terrorism or making speeches that might incite terrorism	Curtailment of freedom of speech
Counter Terrorism Act 2008	The period during which a terrorist suspect can be held without charge or trial was increased from 28 to 42 days (since reduced to 14, see below)	Threat to *habeas corpus,* the principle that people cannot be held for long periods without being brought to trial
Crime and Security Act 2010	This was a general Act concerning crime that relaxed the rules governing police powers of stop and search and seizing or searching property (since tightened up again, see below)	Potential threats to privacy and the protection of private property

Table 10.1 Examples of legislation affecting civil liberties (Continued)

Measure	Key provisions	Nature of the civil liberties threat
Counter Terrorism and Security Act 2015	Restricts movements of those travelling to and from areas where there is terrorist activity, introduces more monitoring of mobile phone and computer messages, and places a responsibility on organisations, notably schools, colleges and universities, to prevent the incitement to terrorism	Freedom of movement is curtailed Monitoring digital messages is an intrusion in privacy There are potential threats to freedom of speech
Current government proposals (yet to be legislated)	The Investigatory Powers Bill 2015–16 will require internet and phone companies to keep records of everyone's browsing history for 12 months. Security services will be able to access them with permission from a senior judge	This threatens personal privacy

Is there any new legal protection for civil liberties?

The picture is not all in one direction. The coalition government did attend to some controversial measures that had been taken at the height of the terrorist threat. This was probably the result of Liberal Democrat influence. Two particular laws have been passed in recent years to provide protection for civil liberties:

- **Protection of Freedom Act 2012.** Among several other measures the Act reduced the period during which suspected terrorists can be held without trial to 14 days. In addition, the police can no longer hold DNA, finger prints or other information on people who have not been convicted of a crime. The Act also tightened up on the police's powers of stop and search and the searching of properties.
- **Justice and Security Act 2013.** This Act created safeguards and controls over the activities of MI5, MI6 and GCHQ (General Communications HQ, which monitors international communications). The oversight has been handed over to the **Intelligence and Security Committee of Parliament**. This independent, cross-party committee reports to Parliament, not the government, and checks whether the intelligence and security services are abusing their powers or acting in a way that threatens rights and the rule of law.

A British Bill of Rights?

In the lead-up to the 2015 general election, David Cameron campaigned for Britain to adopt its own Bill of Rights instead of using the European Convention on Human Rights (ECHR). He is supported strongly by his home secretary, Theresa May, and justice secretary, Michael Gove. At first sight this seems reasonable as it will be a safeguard for rights and civil liberties in the UK. However, there are

many who say the proposal will *threaten* civil liberties, not safeguard them. The other main political parties all opposed it, as did campaign groups Liberty and Amnesty International, as well as the UK Commission for Equality and Human Rights and the former Conservative Attorney General, Dominic Grieve.

Why is this proposal so controversial?

Arguments in favour of replacement

It is argued that the current ECHR has a number of drawbacks:

- Its provisions are not in the control of the UK, but the Council of Europe, so it is an artificial statement of rights, not tailored to the needs of the UK.
- It places too much jurisdiction in the hands of the European Court of Human Rights in Strasbourg, i.e. of unaccountable European judges who may not be interested in the UK's particular circumstances.
- It does not give the UK Parliament and government the flexibility to adjust UK rights according to circumstances, such as terrorism, asylum applications and crime in general. In particular, critics say, it has reduced the UK government's ability to deal with asylum seekers, the deportation of terrorists and the questioning of terrorist suspects. The European Court has also interfered with how the UK deals with prisoners in general.
- It does not give the community as a whole sufficient rights to be protected against crime and terrorism.

Arguments against replacement

It is argued that a British Bill of Rights would be a threat because:

- It would give too much power to the UK government, with a temporary parliamentary majority, to remove some rights, for example in the interests of anti-terrorism or anti-crime measures.
- It would put the UK out of step with the rest of Europe and jeopardise the country's reputation for rights protection.
- It would cause great confusion over rights, as Britain remains a signatory to the European Convention on Human Rights.

Box 10.1   Mark Hammond on a British Bill of Rights

Mark Hammond, the chief executive of the Commission for Equality and Human Rights, commenting on the proposal for a British Bill of Rights to replace the Human Rights Act (ECHR):

> Our view is that any changes to our current human rights framework should not water down the protections in the Human Rights Act. In the year we celebrate the birth of our fundamental freedoms through Magna Carta, it would be a bitter irony to weaken them. We are at a crossroads for human rights. One path risks undermining and diminishing our influence and status as a global leader in human rights and civil liberties. The other path will safeguard both our reputation for fairness and moral authority when confronting human rights abroad.

Source: Letter to Parliament, March 2015

A compromise

As the new government took office it became apparent to David Cameron that if he proposed to replace the ECHR with a British Bill of Rights the measure would not get through Parliament, such is the opposition. A compromise has therefore been proposed. This suggests that there should be a new British Bill of Rights, binding on government and Parliament, but that the ECHR should also be retained, but not be binding on government and Parliament. While this appears to deal with the problems, it too has been widely criticised for being utterly confusing. Under what circumstances would the Bill of Rights be binding, and under what circumstances would judges enforce the ECHR?

Box 10.2 **Michael Gove on a British Bill of Rights**

Michael Gove, justice secretary, speaking in support of replacing the ECHR with a British Bill of Rights:

> What I'm interested in is making sure we have the right system for individuals in this country to have their liberties protected and I think one of the problems that has arisen is that since the Human Rights Act passed into law the interpretation of the European Convention on Human Rights by Strasbourg judges and the way that interpretation has affected our own law hasn't worked in the interests of freedom and liberty in the way that the majority of people in the House of Commons now would have liked.

Source: *Daily Mail*, 6 July 2015

The threat from technology

Looking further into the future, technological developments, notably the internet, mobile phone advances and general surveillance, may also present a threat to our civil liberties. The main issues are:

- It is now possible to trace people's movements through mobile phone records, use of oyster card systems and surveillance cameras. This may be seen as a potential infringement of our privacy.
- It is possible to monitor people's usage of the internet and social media including e-mails and mobile phones (mainly texts), as well as our purchasing habits. This may not be particularly harmful if used for commercial purposes (e.g. cookies), but if it becomes accessible to the state there may be some abuses. For example, it may be used as a means of curbing freedom of speech in the future.
- Access to our online financial dealings may well be used for legitimate reasons by the tax authorities, anti-terrorism forces and the police tracing the proceeds of crime, but it also opens up the possibility of other intrusions into privacy.
- The collection of medical details through complex computer data retrieval systems, including DNA, is also seen as a potential intrusion into our lives.

The issue about technology is not necessarily how it is used now, or how it is used to combat general crime and terrorism, but how it might *potentially* be used by the state in the future. To exacerbate the problem, much technology does not recognise national borders and jurisdictions, so it would be difficult to control without international safeguards.

What are the safeguards?

The good news for those who are concerned about the erosion of civil liberties is that there are a number of systems and institutions whose role is to protect our civil liberties. Among them are:

- **The rule of law.** This is well established in the UK and is a fundamental principle of law. Governments are not above the law and all individuals and groups must be treated equally under the law. Any breach of the principle can be struck down by the courts.
- **The judiciary is independent.** This is especially true since the establishment of the UK's Supreme Court by the **Constitutional Reform Act 2005**. This guarantees a safeguard that, if the state or any of its servants seek to curtail our civil liberties, the courts have the independent power to stop them.
- **The ECHR.** The UK is subject to the European Convention on Human Rights which is established through most of Europe and is out of the control of the UK government. This guarantees civil liberties and is enforced by the independent UK judiciary.
- **Pressure groups.** There is a range of well-resourced pressure groups which monitor dangers to civil liberties, publicise abuses and campaign against them. Among them are **Liberty**, the **British Institute of Human Rights** and **Amnesty International**.
- **Parliamentary sovereignty.** It is one of the roles of both houses of parliament in the UK to check the power of government. The House of Lords in particular, because it is not subject to a government majority, is active in safeguarding rights when legislation or government actions threaten them.

Summary

Whatever the outcome of the various arguments about our rights, there is no doubt that the greatest threat to civil liberties in the UK comes not from dictatorial government, but from the need to deal firmly with terrorists, illegal migrants, serious criminals and asylum seekers. There will always be tension between those who wish to preserve civil liberties at all costs, and those who recognise that sometimes they must be set aside in the interest of peace and national security. The current debate about a British Bill of Rights is not a dry discussion among lawyers, it is a fundamental conflict about who is in the best position to control civil liberties and who should be the main guardians of those liberties — neutral European judges, neutral UK judges, Parliament or government.

Exam focus

To consolidate your knowledge of this chapter, answer the following questions:

1 What is meant by the term 'civil liberties'?
2 In what ways are civil liberties protected in the UK?
3 To what extent can UK judges protect civil liberties?
4 Explain the main current threats to civil liberties.
5 Explain how the responsibilities of government may conflict with the protection of civil liberties and human rights.
6 Why is the issue of a British Bill of Rights so controversial?